abc...

Sometimes back east in Toronto or Ottawa, I hear people say, "Hey, are you going to 'Van' this year?"... and I can't help but shake my head and wonder. In Vancouver there is *East Van* and *North Van* and *West Van,* but never merely Van. Calling Vancouver "Van" is like calling San Francisco "Frisco" or Las Vegas "Vegas." No—it's worse than that—it's like calling Portland "Portl."

Also, people from the South American nation of Colombia are called Colombians. People from B.C. are called British Columbians. It's just a vowel, we know, but we care.

Backlot North

A few years ago I went to see a Hollywood thriller which was partly filmed in front of my father's office building in North Vancouver. In the movie, North Vancouver was "Boulder, Colorado," and throughout the movie Vancouver doubled as Seattle, Denver, New Orleans and a few other cities, none of them Vancouver. The thing is, Vancouver can neatly morph into just about any North American city save for those in the American Southwest, and possibly Miami. Legend has it that somewhere in the city there exists a mythical prop warehouse filled with nothing but *Seattle Post-Intelligencer* paper boxes, Denver Broncos billboards and extremely lifelike fake palm trees.

Once, in Helsinki, I was in a hotel where the TV had six channels. Five were showing made-in-Vancouver cable films, and the sixth was CNN. I phoned my mom and we watched CNN simultaneously. It sort of felt like home.

Vancouver feels like a functioning model of how American cities and neighbourhoods were *supposed* to have functioned in 1961. This is, of course, part of the reason why TV and movie filming here is so popular and easy to do. Many of the factors that stripped the innocence away from other cities never occurred here: freeways were never built and a soul-free edge city never arose because Vancouver has no edge. It hits the mountains on one side, the ocean on the other and the U.S. border on the third, so land use has always remained somewhat conservative.

Vancouver is North America's third-largest film and TV production centre after Los Angeles and New York. The province's generous tax laws and talented infrastructure also keep the filming happening despite the dollar's recent rise. But you don't hear people discussing local filming too much, and it doesn't seep into daily life the way it does in Los Angeles.

In 2006 a movie I wrote, *Everything's Gone Green,* was set and filmed in Vancouver. In 2007 we shot and set a thirteen-episode series I created here in Vancouver, too. I noted that even in that one intervening year I witnessed a subtle but distinct shift in the way Vancouverites view made-in-Vancouver projects. The fact that Vancouver increasingly gets to be itself in film and TV has given the city a new confidence, and we no longer feel so conflicted about the borderline-cheesy movies-of-the-week and made-for-cable films shot here in which we disguise the city as Seattle, Portland, Chicago ... and so forth.

City of Glass

Douglas Coupland's **Vancouver**
Revised Edition

 Douglas & McIntyre

D&M Publishers Inc.
Vancouver/Toronto/Berkeley

City of Glass

Douglas Coupland's **Vancouver**
Revised Edition

To my parents, who had the genius to point their Conestoga wagons westward back in 1965.

Thanks to the many people who helped this book along, especially Jen Eby for her talent and her hard work and good cheer amid so many deadlines.

Also thanks to Mr. Ian Verchère for writing about mountain biking in this revised edition. Ian is the author of a terrific book on Whistler called *V0N 1B0* (that's Whistler's postal code).

Copyright © 2009 by Douglas Coupland

09 10 11 12 13 5 4 3 2 1

Douglas & McIntyre
A division of D&M Publishers Inc.
2323 Quebec Street, Suite 201
Vancouver BC Canada V5T 4S7
www.douglas-mcintyre.com

Library and Archives Canada Cataloguing in Publication

Coupland, Douglas
     City of glass : Douglas Coupland's Vancouver. — Rev. ed.

ISBN 978-1-55365-359-2

     1. Vancouver (B.C.). 2. Vancouver (B.C.) — Pictorial works.
I. Title.
FC3847.3.C68 2009   971.1'33   C2009-900425-9

Editing by Saeko Usukawa, Corky McIntyre
Cover design by Jen Eby
Text design by Steedman Design, Jen Eby
Map design by Robin Mitchell
Printed and bound in China by C&C Offset Printing Co. Ltd.
Printed on acid-free paper
Distributed in the U.S. by Publishers Group West

We gratefully acknowledge the financial support of the Canada Council for the Arts, the British Columbia Arts Council, the Province of British Columbia through the Book Publishing Tax Credit and the Government of Canada through the Book Publishing Industry Development Program (BPIDP) for our publishing activities.

Here's a still from the film *Everything's Gone Green*. Actor Paulo Costanzo stands in front of a fake beached grey whale. The carcass was the single most expensive production item in the movie, but the scene was important and was based on my own real life experience where I heard on the radio that a whale had beached itself near Engish Bay. Hundreds of Vancouverites did the same thing as me, and walking up to it and touching it was almost holy.

BC Ferries

To get to Vancouver Island or any of the other small beautiful islands between there and Vancouver, most people take BC Ferries, and many of us have a ferry schedule taped to the fridge. The ferry is technically what you might call a "frozen freeway"—it's all of the people and cars you would have met if there were a freeway between here and the island. Ferries are wonderfully democratic and to walk the deck of one is to garner a good cross-sectional view of society: bureaucrats, loggers, students, retirees with their Winnebagos and always lots of sugar-fuelled kids.

Warning: a major part of the ferry experience involves waiting; that's because it's government-subsidized and, in a way, the slow pace is part of the marine Zen. A one-sailing wait is annoying but tolerable. A two-sailing wait is blood-boiling and involves much self-blame for having chosen a bad departure time, plus a free-floating anger at a society that allows for the possibility of a two-ferry wait to even exist. A three-sailing wait I've never done, but I'm sure many crimes have been committed in its wake, and only the iciest-blooded of judges would feel no compassion for the three-sailing waiter.

The proper protocol for being on a ferry is this: the moment after you've locked your car (assuming you drove on), you rush like mad up to the cafeteria lineup and stand there for a goodly amount of time waiting to buy french fries. Red Jell-O cubes are also sold.

In spite of all the drawbacks, most Vancouverites have fond ferry memories. The ride is relaxing, and for some it's a rare chance to mix with fellow British Columbians. Seagulls love the ferries, too, and much fun can be had with a plate of french fries, tossing them up into the air into their beaks. The gulls fly at the same speed as the ferry, thus making them seem motionless. Then the other gulls catch on and it gets really brutal as they bite each other's feet, all to get your french fries. It's carnage and it really makes you rethink all your preconceptions about birds.

Beads & Granola

Hippies may be as archaic as flappers, but they did lots of good things for Vancouver. Vancouver was Canada's San Francisco–style alternative destination, with much of the scene centred along West 4th Avenue. My own memories of the period are naturally very sketchy, but then, as it turns out, so are the memories of the people who were there. It was all very groovy and Deadheady, and it couldn't disappear fast enough as far as I was concerned. But that's just me, and I'm the first to admit that much of what defines Vancouver comes from the great hippie push: no freeways, Greenpeace, regional cuisine and fusion foods, utopian urban planning schemes, plus a heady sense of personal freedom that is slightly absent in other cities.

People from back east have held on to the notion of Vancouver being a hippie theme park long past the point when that might have been construed as even slightly true. The picture of Vancouver as beads-and-granola is outdated, but having lived back east and having family out there, all I can say is that they're somewhat *relieved,* however reluctant they may be to admit it, that there exists an alternative to the buttoned-down lives they lead there. Enough said. Hey guys—come and visit!

When I was growing up, many of my schoolteachers were Children of '68, and they tried their hardest to spread their message. But, of course, I and my cohorts ended up as a generation (*Doug, don't say it*) of computer-embracing, punk-rock pragmatists in response to the dippiness of the sixties. But the hippies might take heart that the best of what they believed valuable was, in the end, passed on to the khaki-loving kids who followed them. Many sitcoms and Sunday paper think-pieces on the subject have appeared, so the subject need not be discussed further. But as comedienne Sandra Bernhard has said, on a clear night, you can hear Joni up in the canyons knitting a shawl.

Bellingham & the Border

In the not-so-distant past, the typical Vancouver mother might visit Bellingham maybe twice a year to shop, and in recent years the shopping largely shifted to the Bellis Fair Mall and the factory outlets along I-5. Things really are cheaper in the U.S. It was also not uncommon to head down to Seattle for a day trip, but those day trips are now largely memories, as Vancouverites no longer view Seattle as a day trip. Even day shopping in Bellingham, bargains notwithstanding, doesn't seem like the fun day out it once was. Most Vancouverites have horror stories involving U.S. border crossing guards—their meanness, their anger, their hostility and their paranoia. Who needs it? Last month I was near a border crossing and there were no lineups, so I thought I'd pop across and go grocery shopping like the old days. Bad idea. The guard was so nasty and pointlessly rude that I turned around and came right back home. Are Americans even aware that this is the face they uniformly present to the world? It's spooky.

And it's not just going into the U.S. that's a bitch; coming back home can be just as nasty. I've noticed that pretty much everybody has a pet border superstition. The most common one is that, returning to Canada, you don't want to get the mythical Young Woman Out To Prove She Can Be As Tough As Any Man. Its corollary superstition is to try to get The Tired Old Guy Who's Seen It All and Only Has Two Weeks Left Until Retirement. He'll let you get away with anything.

Everybody always brings (smuggles, really) back way more than they declare, and everybody knows the falsetto their voice hits as they declare, "Oh, maybe fifty bucks in groceries and a tank of gas." Nobody wants the dreaded Strip Search Room, or possibly worse, Those Miserable Bastards Who'll Rip Up Your Car Leaving You With a Pile of Metal and You Have No Legal Recourse Whatsoever. The truth is actually more boring. Canada's bankrupt and needs all the money it can get. In the end, it's easier to declare the lot and pay the stinking $5.63 tax. That, of course, means standing in the tax lineup which is always long and always slow. But this is outweighed by the elation of smuggling back twenty pounds of Jack cheese, four hundred frozen bacon-rolled scallops and a pile of Liz Claiborne towels.

Word of advice: if you have to drive through the border either way, check the radio station to see which crossing has the smallest lineup: AM 730 does so every few minutes. Make the wrong choice of border crossing and you can easily waste up to an hour or two (or three!) in a lineup while others a few kilometres away are zooming through.

The Big One

Richmond is the part of town located on the flat Fraser River delta area south of the airport. Locals call it "Ditchmond," but only they get to call it that. One thing you need to know about visiting Richmond is that once you go there, you will get lost. This is not a joke. You. Will. Get. Lost. This is a fact and any Vancouverite reading these words knows exactly what I mean. You can't see the mountains from Richmond, so all of your bearings are lost. The roads all look the same, and if you make one wrong turn—and you will—it's curtains. Enjoy!

Richmond used to be pumpkin, corn, strawberry and blueberry fields up until recent decades. Now, it's one great big condominium, which is not necessarily a bad thing, except that, when the Big One comes—and it *will* come—the whole place will sink into soil that has liquefied into chocolate pudding, just like San Francisco's Marina District in 1989.

Vancouver doesn't get the same number of earthquakes as California, but we're part of the same tectonic system. The fact that there hasn't been an earthquake in a while only means that the one we do get will be huge. The city has been quietly seismically upgrading its water and bridge systems over the past few years. The city *knows*.

Richmond is popular with Vancouver's Asian community because its name contains the word "rich," and hence is lucky. I'm not making this up. My Asian friends also tell me that they like the fact the airport is nearby and that their grandparents are suspicious of bridges, which, during times of war, tend to be destroyed—"And then where does that leave you?" Asian culture is ancient, and they know stuff we can't even imagine. During the Great War of 2087, Richmond might well be the place to be.

As an added note, shopping is the big deal in Richmond, and possibly the area's most intriguing aspect is the Yaohan (pronounced *yoe-han*), which is an Asian supermall with Asian everything for sale. From there, you can take a series of IQ-testing cloverleafs to head toward Ikea and the big-box stores nearby, all of which will become glorious colourful rubble within ten seconds some future rainy afternoon.

Richmond's Aberdeen Centre, Vancouver's Asian supermall.

Birds

The provincial bird of B.C. is the Steller's Jay. It's a deep dazzling Prussian blue colour with a black crest and black markings. It's related to both the crow and the eastern bluebird, and its personality is unmistakable. Nearly everybody in the tree-filled suburbs is familiar with this, the most emotionally transparent of birds, whose greatest desire is the unshelled roasted peanut. *Greed! Pettiness! Energy! Curiosity!* It just can't help itself, and that's why we love it, even as it invites itself to our alpine picnics or leaves peanut shells in our drainpipes, causing big plug-ups. But the Steller's Jay does tend to avoid downtown, so if you can make it into the suburbs to see it, it's worth the trek.

Vancouver also has its share of bald eagles, some of which can be seen soaring above the Cypress Bowl road, looking for pre-flattened "road snacks." Eagles, despite their appearance on U.S. money and their threateningly dramatic appearance, can also be viewed as seagulls with a good hairdo. I grew up thinking that they were on the cusp of extinction, but now suddenly they're everywhere. In early spring, bald eagles swarm by the hundreds in Brackendale, which is on the road to Whistler, and throughout the year they circle the bluff near the spit-road that leads out to the BC Ferries terminal at Tsawwassen.

In Stanley Park, there are hundreds of Canada geese. Sometimes during the hatching season and shortly thereafter, these geese (for reasons we humans will never fully fathom) need to waddle with dignity across the Lions Gate Causeway, *particularly* at rush hour. Protocol demands that traffic stop and the geese be allowed to cross with a smile and a wave.

And, of course, there are the seagulls—what can I say? They're noisy, they're slightly brash, like an Australian rugby team one hour into a kegger, but they do keep our streets clear of fast-food refuse.

Cantonese

The city that Vancouver most closely resembles, if it can be said to resemble any other at all, is Honolulu, which also has a lot of people squished into a small area bordered by mountains, hyperinflated real estate values, a sense of disconnection from the rest of the world and, not least, a racial and ethnic mix of Natives, Europeans and Asians.

Statistics vary, but roughly one-quarter of Vancouverites speak Chinese at home. Punjabi and Vietnamese are second and third, with French a distant ninth, after Italian. To Americans and Europeans, this demographic mix is startling and seems almost like a "parallel-universe." *What if history had been rerouted in other ways? What if the continent had been settled from the west to the east, instead of from east to west?*

I once took a night course in Cantonese, thinking it would be like Japanese, and boy was I wrong—it is *much* harder than Japanese. But the most intriguing thing about the class was the mix of students. They were largely non-Asian men and women marrying into Cantonese-speaking households. One of them was a punk with a pierced nose and orange mohawk, learning to count to ten and to name the days of the week. Afterward, his girlfriend and future granny would come to pick him up, and granny would drill her future grandson-in-law like a marine sergeant, making darned sure he used only the honorific form for addressing her.

Most Vancouverites, Asian or not, were concerned that the British handover of Hong Kong to China in 1999 was going to be a disaster. Consequently, the supply of money that might have gone into maintaining a certain kind of boom in Vancouver ground to a halt, but to be honest, everybody breathed a sigh of relief, because there was too much happening too quickly and we all needed some digestion time.

Now, with the economy the way it is, Vancouver real estate rides and sinks with the fortunes of the Pacific economy. It remains the most enigmatic and unpredictable of all of North America's housing markets, but as my accountant says, "As long as more people are coming into a city than leaving it, it's pretty hard to go wrong."

溫哥華 Vancouver as written in Cantonese

Chinatown

In fifth grade, I'd take the buses down to Chinatown on rainy Saturdays, by myself mostly, and absorb the neighbourhood's signature aroma of ginseng, mothballs and dried fish, as well as its (to a fifth grader) exotic tableaux of pigs' heads, bamboo knick-knacks and unbelievably inexpensive paper products. The noise! The colour! And yes, all the clichés! But what fascinating clichés.

Later, during art school, the alleys of Chinatown were a true Klondike of found beauty—the crates and cardboards and packing papers imprinted with their faraway legends. To this day, I find that if a person doesn't want to walk through Chinatown's alleys prowling for odd bits of loveliness, then I really have to question, just who is this person?

Chinatown has never lost its appeal for me, but the historical Chinatown represents only one specific version of Sino-Canadian identity—and it's not one that all Chinese Canadians embrace. Just as Europe embraces Norway, Greece and Ireland, China has many takes on Chineseness. Newer nodes of Chineseness have sprung up, most notably in Richmond and in the Kerrisdale neighbourhood. Downtown's Chinatown went through a big cleanup and boom during the 1980s and early 1990s, but thereafter the money moved away to suburbia; now it has reverted back to its less go-go cozier self. And the alleys are as good as ever.

Colours

Vancouver is obviously the greenest of cities, and you can assemble a varied green palette using the following species: **cedar, fir, rhododendron, vine maple.**

Along with greenery, no Vancouver plant-life palette would be complete without the delicate pink of all **blossom** types and the lush gentle tones of the **Japanese split-leaf maple.** And, of course, there are **mussels**—in their own way a kind of marine vegetation—which loan their distinctive deep blue colour to the city.

The **sky** in Vancouver has its own distinct tinge, just like London or Los Angeles—a milky grey colour that melts onto the steel blue mountain slopes. When watching TV movies, locals can almost always spot the ones filmed here simply because of the quality of the light.

Vancouver is a rainy city, so its buildings leak. This sounds simple. *However,* in the 1980s, the government decided to make the city's new buildings completely leak proof and enacted all sorts of regulations to ensure this. The scheme

cedar

fir

rhododendron

vine maple

plum blossom

japanese maple

mussel

sky

orange tarp

blue tarp

teal fleece

glass

backfired dismally, making houses more intractably and expensively leaky, and bankrupting more than a few families. The litigation will go on forever.

A side effect of this boneheaded decision is that the city's buildings abound with **plastic tarps** of either cheerful orange or sunshiny blue. These festive buntings are everywhere and, when divorced from their sinister implications, can look cheerful indeed. Recently, when I had lunch with a friend in the revolving restaurant at the Empire Landmark, we had a contest to see who could spot the most tarps. Neither of us won, because even as the bill arrived, we were still spotting them.

The colour teal is also big in Vancouver. The very word "teal" evokes memories of, say, 1992—but it has become a Vancouver classic. This is in large part due to the **fleece** industry.

Another Vancouver favourite is the colour of **glass**—hence the title of this book—but that's a section on its own.

Couples

Mixed-ancestry marriages are common in Vancouver in a way matched only, perhaps, by Rio de Janeiro. Pretty well everyone in Vancouver is either in a mixed-ancestry relationship or has several coupled friends who are. No one thinks about it too much, and it only ever seems like a big deal when people from outside the city express surprise. In a poetic way, it feels as if human history, which began in Asia and moved ever westward across the centuries, is now making the final connection by hooking up western North America with Asia. Or ... it's almost impossible to say much more on the subject, because what is there to say? It's just a part of Vancouver life, like the air: beautiful and clean and scented with salt water and plum blossoms.

Dim Sum

Dim sum is a tapas-like Chinese meal at which little trolleys carrying various treats are wheeled past your table for you to pick and choose. Many non-Asian Vancouverites remember the first time the lid was removed to reveal steamed chicken feet—quite a delicacy though I have yet to muster the courage to eat one. Dim sum is one of those things, like karaoke, which were exotic and foreign a few years ago, and which are now almost fully integrated into the city's fabric. (Fun fact: Many new homes built for the city's Asian community have karaoke rooms.) It can feel really odd if you're not Chinese to walk into a huge Chinese restaurant bustling with a dozen families seated at large round tables, but just dive in and you'll get used to it very quickly.

Dim sum food is generally pretty good, but it's also quite mysterious in name (selections arrive nameless) as well as in contents ... steamed pork balls spring to mind, though when I eat them I remind myself I eat hot dogs at hockey games, too.

England's Dreaming

I grew up in a part of Vancouver called the British Properties, up on Hollyburn Mountain on the North Shore. It was a suburban subdivision begun in the 1930s by Britain's Guinness family, who bought the land for something like $1.95 at the turn of the century. They then built Lions Gate Bridge in 1938, to link this land to the downtown core.

During the 1960s and 1970s, there was probably no more middle-class place on Earth than the British Properties. In spite of this, the suburb was typecast as Martini Hill. If only the typecasters knew how wrong they were. Back then, the norm was four kids, a Ford, a Volvo and a sheepdog. The big irony is that the British Properties really are Martini Hill these days, as well as the city's favourite location for marijuana grow operations. But most people don't even think about the Properties any more.

Anyway, a few years back, I ended up spending a weekend at a Guinness castle in Ireland. This sounds much grander than it really was—chilly, rooms painted odd colours, taxidermied bits of endangered species—quite mad and sad. Abounding on the walls were photos of fat old lords with guns, standing behind hundreds of dead birds and animals—to be expected, I suppose. But then I looked at the names of the places—Biddesden, Hadden, Pyrford, Elveden—and realized that all the streets around where I'd grown up were named after these dead rich British guys or their estates or their black Labradors or what have you. And then I had this almost psychic vision of these fat old rich guys sitting around a fire in a London club one night seventy years ago naming all the British Properties' streets and getting big chuckles and ha-has as they named a street after "the bartender Fruity killed when he got sloshed and stole Lady Quimby's electric car at Badminton last summer and drove it into the tables beside the croquet pitch." Or, "Old Nanny Kenwood, *such* a dear." The *contempt* these men must have felt for the provincial yokels who'd never know that the street they lived on was christened after the in-joke name for the Guinness family loo, or a prized spaniel bitch.

England's relationship to Vancouver isn't all tea and crumpets. The English pretty much sucked all they could out of Vancouver for the first many decades of the twentieth century: natural resources, men to fight their battles, rents and development profits. We were a branch plant cynically manipulated from afar. The English may not own Vancouver now but Anglophilia remains. For instance, all those developments you see above the highway on the North Shore are monster houses on streets with English names like Canterbury, Marlow and Whitby—names intended to evoke "elegance" and "refinement," no matter that they're not. I hope someday there's a mass revolt and the land gets taken back, but that kind of thing never happens. So build away, lads.

The ESL Pot Holiday

In the 1990s, downtown Vancouver witnessed a massive influx of Japanese teenagers, jet-lagged and giddy from having recently escaped straitlaced Japan. Technically many of them were here to study English, but what they were really doing in Vancouver was taking lavish and inexpensive pot holidays.

The Japanese were the first wave and have now been followed by successive waves of Asian young people whose home countries have draconian drug laws. That would explain the existence of Korean supermarkets in the core of the city as well as scores of Japanese restaurants just about everywhere.

Canadian immigration laws are such that a student coming to attend a "school" in Canada has to have a visa. However, there are no rules about attendance and an astonishing number of "students" simply don't attend, and then renew their visas for the school down the block for the following year. Scam!

Pot aside, for these young people, Vancouver is an affordable, chaperone-free idyll before they enter Asia's corporate meat grinder. Here, they get to wear wacky outfits, sleep in, drink too much, get violently homesick and, oddly, will never speak an English word if they can help it. You, the outsider, may look at these colourful creatures, but there's not much point in saying hello, as they simply will not interact with locals—*period*—though I really wish they would, because I think they'd have some interesting ideas. *Hey! You guys! Talk or something!*

90年代では、都心のバンクーバーは最近脱出することから厳格な日本をジェット機遅れた、めまいがする日本のティーネージャーの大きい流入を目撃した。厳密にはそのほとんどはここに英語を調査することいたがバンクーバーで実際にしていた何を物惜しみしなく、安価なマリファナの休日を取っていた。

　　　日本人は最初の波、故国に厳密な薬剤の法律があるアジア若者達の連続的な波に今先行してしまった。それは都市のコアの韓国のスーパーマーケットの存在、またたくさんの日本食料理店をちょうど約どこでも説明する。

　　　カナダの移住の法律はカナダのEschoolに出席することを来ている学生に査証がなければならないことそのような物である。ただし、出席についての規則がないし、Estudentsの驚くほど番号は単に出席しないし、次に次の年のブロックの下の学校のための査証に更新する。詐欺!

　　　わきマリファナは、これらの若者達のために、バンクーバーそれらがアジアの団体の肉挽き器を入力する前に現実的な、付き添いなしの牧歌である。ここでは、それらはそれを助けてもいければ風変りな用品類を身に着けることを得、スリープの状態であり、あまりを飲み、激しくホームシックになり、そして、異様に、決して英国ワードを話さない。私が実際に望む支部ピリオドけれどもの局外者、これらの多彩な創造物を見る挨拶に多くのポイントがない、と単に相互に作用していないのでことを、私が考えるのである興味深い考えを有することを。ちょっと! 貴方達! 話または何か!

Amusingly bad translation (of facing page) courtesy of the Internet.

Expo 86

In 1986, Vancouver hosted a world's fair which had the theme "A World in Motion." A lot of people came to see it—about 35 million, but if I ever design a world's fair, I'm going to ensure it has a Used Book pavilion and a Flea Market pavilion. The fair had a mascot named Expo Ernie (gag) who looked like he was designed by somebody's nephew over the weekend for $125.00. But the event did put Vancouver on people's radar, and it's also the location of that famous shot of Charles and Diana where you could finally tell for sure that they hated each other.

Many Expo visitors developed what was euphemistically called "hiker's rash" on their legs. This was actually caused by fumes from the toxic waste beneath the pavement, which, once the fair was over, created a bureaucratic and political fiasco. This toxic industrial sludge had to be dug up and incinerated, truckload by truckload, before any construction could begin. The City of Tomorrow—*the city of glass*—that was to appear on the site took a decade to even begin and, only now, over twenty years later, is fulfilling the promises made before the fair by real estate developers' seductive photos.

Ｆeng Shui

You've heard the term used but you're probably unsure of what it means. In general, a place with good feng shui has "good vibes." If a place feels wrong—and we've all walked into rooms that are slightly creepy—then the room usually has bad feng shui. When Vancouverites describe living spaces, the words "feng shui" are used interchangeably with "vibe."

Feng shui has rules, but only a few Chinese masters know what they are. Books offer conflicting ideologies ("the space should *flowwwwww*" or "flow is to be avoided at all costs"), but Cantonese newcomers to Vancouver take it very seriously, and there are professional feng shui-ifiers available should one be required.

Fleece

Fleece is, along with Gore-Tex, neoprene, Velcro, laminated fibres and khaki, Vancouver's official fabric. It's lightweight, suitable for both alpine and marine activities, handles water like a charm, and is warm. Only drawback: when it starts pilling, it can look kind of scary. Fleece is just a part of an overall outdoorsy look pioneered in Vancouver, a hiking-boot-and-nylon-parka aesthetic created unintentionally during the 1970s and 1980s. In recent years this outdoorsy sensibility has interbred with the yoga-based fashion sensibility—light fabrics, locking zippers and the city's key fashion status symbol: thumb holes on the sleeves. Local brands gone global include Arc'teryx and Lululemon.

   The most famous outdoor outlet is Mountain Equipment Co-op, and their stores are staffed and shopped in exclusively by people in ferocious health with dewy complexions. In the same way you might clean up the house before the maid arrives, you dress more athletically before shopping there so as not to feel like a complete slug.

   The good thing is that no matter how out of shape you are, don the outdoorsy togs and you'll look like the embodiment of health.

Food Porn

Vancouverites are completely spoiled when it comes to food. Pretty much anything you can eat is grown close by or is readily available to the city's residents, and Vancouver's cuisine easily matches that of Sydney or San Francisco. Take something like sushi. I've lived in Japan a few times, and during these stints I've noticed that the Japanese don't really eat all that much sushi. I asked about this, and they said it was only for special occasions, the same way North Americans only roast turkeys a couple of times a year. So I can only imagine how strange the Japanese find it that Vancouverites eat sushi both often and in large quantities, selling it even at gas stations. It must be much like going to, say, France, and finding that the French eat Christmas dinner twenty-five times a year.

There are scores of sushi restaurants in Vancouver, some of which are amazing and which the Japanese admit are even better than their own, lots of pretty good ones and, yes, a few stinkers. Pretty much all Vancouverites will eat a tuna, salmon or eel sushi without quibbling. They're the sushi flavour equivalents of chocolate, strawberry and vanilla. And once you've eaten sushi, it's pretty hard to go back to eating canned tuna. Think about it: on the one hand, with sushi, you have this fresh, pink yummy stuff called fresh tuna—and on the other hand, you have a can of this stuff which is also "tuna" but which happens to be beige, flaky and ... not very tuna-y.

Then there's the 100-Mile Diet, the first true diet craze of the 21st century, originated in Vancouver. But to call it a craze is wrong—what it is is a quick wake-up slap on the face, calling for people to be less lazy in their approach to food and try to keep it local. Can you eat only food that originates within a hundred miles of your home? Probably not, but in making the effort—establishing links with farmers' markets, surfing the Internet, buying in bulk and maybe starting a garden of your own—you can wean yourself off of corporate diets and into far healthier foodstuffs, which almost by accident tend to be oddly gourmet. Check out Granville Island, Trout Lake farmers' market, or go one further and head out into the Fraser Valley and meet some farmers, many of whom are quite happy to take you on tours of their operations. Just knock.

Greenpeace

Vancouver isn't really a global corporate headquarters to much of anything. Instead, it's a bedroom community to the global meritocracy—a clan that tends to be morally and socially disengaged from local political issues. Perhaps because of the city's lack of distinct corporate entities, it is, along with many cities of the so-called Cascadia region, a wellspring of dissent against the forces of bland global corporate nothingness. The sight of U.S. riot troops tear-gassing young people out of a burning Seattle downtown core during the 1999 WTO meeting set a young Vancouverite's heart aflutter with noble thoughts.

In this same vein, it was in a Vancouver basement, in September 1971, that Greenpeace was founded in response to the U.S. government's intended detonation, on the Alaskan island of Amchitka, of a Spartan missile warhead of between four and five megatons at the bottom of a 2.4-kilometre (1.5-mile) vertical shaft. The blast was labelled "Cannikin," and it took place on the afternoon of November 6. I was in a McDonald's restaurant for my first time, at the corner of Pemberton and Marine Drive in North Van, frightened beyond medical retrieval, waiting for the world to end in a blizzard of melting Hamburglars. The detonation, unnoticed everywhere else on the planet, electrified two Vancouver generations. Greenpeace went forth from fringe obscurity to radicalize much of the rest of the planet.

In general, Big is suspect. Vancouver distrusts Big. We don't want Big. Big is to be fought. The country's prime minister visits Vancouver as little as possible—and we all know it. During those rare visits, elaborate efforts are made to ensure that the prime minister is neither egged nor ignored. It's the way that it's been for all of the city's life.

Above I helped clean up this 1973 oil spill on West Vancouver's gentle and unassuming Ambleside beach. I was eleven at the time and didn't sleep for a week afterward. Photo by Glenn Baglo, *Vancouver Sun*

Grouse Mountain

In 1967 my father came home from a hunting trip with a deer strapped to the trunk of his Fairlane. Although we lived in the suburbs of West Van then, the appearance of a deer on a car's trunk seemed neither improper nor implausible. Within 450 metres (500 yards) of our house's front door was a chain-link fence that separates West Vancouver from what lies on the other side, which is, with the exception of the odd power line, logging road or train track, a raw wilderness. My parents still live near that house, and when visitors come from out of town, I take them up the Grouse Mountain SkyRide and point it out while riding in the gondola. I also point out the wilderness to the north—just a quick scoot over the fence—and visitors say, "Geez, Doug, I thought you were just being *metaphorical* about the wilderness ..." They then stand and gawk at the Capilano Valley. The valley was logged long ago, so it's all second growth, but it can pass for wilderness nonetheless. *Boomp!*—the gondola berths at the top. The snow is thick; the nearby peaks loom, too steep to log or otherwise modify. This is where it dawns, on everybody from newcomers to season's ticket holders, that we live in a place that really has no equivalent anywhere else on Earth.

As teenagers, bored out of our minds during long summer holidays, we'd cable up Grouse Mountain and walk through the blueberry and salmonberry scrub looking for money that skiers had dropped in the rocks beneath the chairlifts. The most we ever found was a two-dollar bill and plastic bags filled with desiccated pot, but we *did* see lots of rather fearless blue grouse—so the mountain is aptly named. We bought season's passes for $99.00 back then, when the weather was colder and the winters were longer—and we pretty much lived on the slopes from November to March, on weekends and after school, thanks to nighttime skiing. Not a week goes by now without a night-skiing dream—such a mythical flight-like sensation, to be swooping down the sodium-lit swaths of the runs, young and problemless and pure!

Grouse is open year-round, and not to be missed. The original 1960s James Bond Villain Alpine Retreat has been pasted over with a corny faux–Swiss chalet thingamabob. But the air is thin, the view is spectacular, and the presence of something holy is always just a breath and a glance away, off in the hinterlands.

The Grouse Grind

And while we're on the subject of Grouse Mountain, a few years ago, it dawned on people that the city's biggest singles bar (what a quaint 1970s term) wasn't a bar at all. Instead, the hottest pickup spot in town was actually the 2.8-kilometre (1.8-mile) trail that runs beneath the Grouse Mountain gondola. During the summer months, people dash from their offices, bolt up Capilano Road and Nancy Greene Way, where they doff their work togs and change into sexy hiking gear. And then they walk their brains out. Thursday is the heaviest traffic night. The average time to go up the Grind is just over an hour, but some people, um, how shall we say ... dawdle. Others do it much more quickly, often many times in a row, as well.

The Grind isn't open all year long. In 1998—a phenomenal snow year—a Grinder from Ontario was buried in an avalanche above the gondola's middle tower. The situation was too perilous for rescue parties to retrieve him, and so

for months, Vancouverites looked at the Grind, visible from most of Vancouver, knowing there was this frozen body up there in the snow. It was haunting, and remains for me some sort of central myth of the city—just as, in 1947, when TransCanada Airlines Flight No. 3 crashed just a short hike away from civilization on the North Shore mountains and remained there for fifty years, fifteen skeletons and all, before being accidentally found by municipal workers in 1997. In the futile search for the craft shortly after its disappearance, dozens of leads were followed, including one from Mrs. E. Van Welter of Mayne Island, who found a photo of a woman in the belly of a salmon she was cleaning. Hard to imagine that in, say, Winnipeg or Phoenix.

Grow-Ops

Vancouver's pot is world renowned for its potency. It's a billion times more powerful than anything you smoked in high school or college. Much of this pot comes from grow-ops—indoor hydroponics plantations located in basements. Pretty much every residential block in Vancouver has one, if not several, marijuana grow-ops taking place in one of its houses—way more than you'd ever suspect. With a bit of horticultural panache, a few wits and a bit of wiring to steal electricity from BC Hydro, it's a surefire way to big and quick money. Pot is among B.C.'s five largest industries.

To find a grow-op, look for a house (most likely rented out by unaware dupes) with the lawn un-mown, humidity fogging the window corners, and just one light glowing in a front window. Grow-op owners never think to turn on a second light to make a house look slightly lived in, probably because it'd use even more electricity.

Grow-ops used to be nudged and winked at by the authorities, but there's been a bit of a clampdown recently. The pot scenario changes by the day. One week, the bikers and Vietnamese are taking over the business; the next week, the U.S. has donated millions to help Canada get rid of the stuff.

Probably the RCMP are putting the larger part of their effort into curtailing the massive heroin shipments that arrive in the city via freighters, or tracking down crack, which, along with meth, is taking a pronounced social toll on Vancouver.

But pot? Most Vancouverites basically don't think pot's the real issue and suspect—with whatever accurate level of paranoia—that pot crackdowns have something to do with the Kremlinological machinations of the White House rather than the plant itself.

Hemp, on the other hand, is the non-smokable part of a marijuana plant and is fully legal to own and sell in Canada. I've noticed (and it's a fairly easy observation to make) that the people who make a big deal about buying hemp clothing are also the ones who smoke pot. I've yet to see someone buy hemp clothing and take a "no" stance toward pot. ("Pot is immoral, but oh, those hemp drawstring pants are so darn *flirty!*") I also wonder if people who wear hemp clothes go through airports much, because Sparky the Drug Dog would be on to them in a blink. *Duh!*

All this aside, you can purchase a fine but somewhat locked-in-time fashion wise selection of hemp wear in a number of downtown stores. Americans get the giddiest when they visit these shops. Hemp is so demonized in the U.S. that the hemporium experience must be akin to doing vodka shooters naked on a Salt Lake City street corner at midday. Asian young people visiting the city, on the other hand, dogpile into the hemp shops and clean them out. Remember: even Paul McCartney got busted for pot in Japan.

The Harbour

When I was five, our family was in the car, driving across the Second Narrows Bridge towards the PNE. My older brothers were tormenting me because they could read and I couldn't yet. Just then we were passing the Alberta Wheat Pool, the large grain elevators on the city's east edge. Much of the wheat from the Prairies finds its way out into the world from this Pool, and on its south face were the crimson words "ALBERTA WHEAT POOL," painted 30 metres (100 feet) high. Anyway, my brothers continued to taunt me, and my oldest brother said, "I bet you can't read *that*." I looked at the big red letters and proved him wrong: "It says, *Alberta Wheat Pool.*" At that moment reading clicked in my brain and since then I've read at more or less the same speed. The *Saskatchewan* Wheat Pool is on the opposite side of the harbour. Had we been driving by those grain elevators, I might still be illiterate.

The city's harbour is beloved by Vancouverites, who as a rule tend to love those big piles of pale yellow sulphur on the north shore of Burrard Inlet—the by-product of producing natural gas up the coast. People who *aren't* from Vancouver look at the sulphur piles and say, "*Yuck* ... I thought you guys liked nature." It's a real divider.

Growing up, my friends and I used to be able to sneak onto the sulphur piles on weekends and ski down their slopes—probably not the smartest thing to do—but how could any kid resist? It was all so pure and clean and yellow—with no security guards anywhere.

You used to be able to drive around the port area, but in 2005 it was closed off to all but the people who work there. Thank you, 9-11. But before 2005, you really had to watch out driving around the docks, because there were a lot of people down there moving around things that, er, shouldn't be moved, and they *didn't* want you seeing it.

There's a good probability that your neighbour's stolen 2006 Camry is going to be a Sweet 16 gift for the daughter of a Vladivostock nightclub owner. I once had four truly enraged longshoremen surrounding my old VW Rabbit, when all I was doing was looking for bits of old metal for an art school project. So, beware. I also heard a rumour that the seagulls there are extra mean.

3,400,000 dollar store
vinyl spatulas

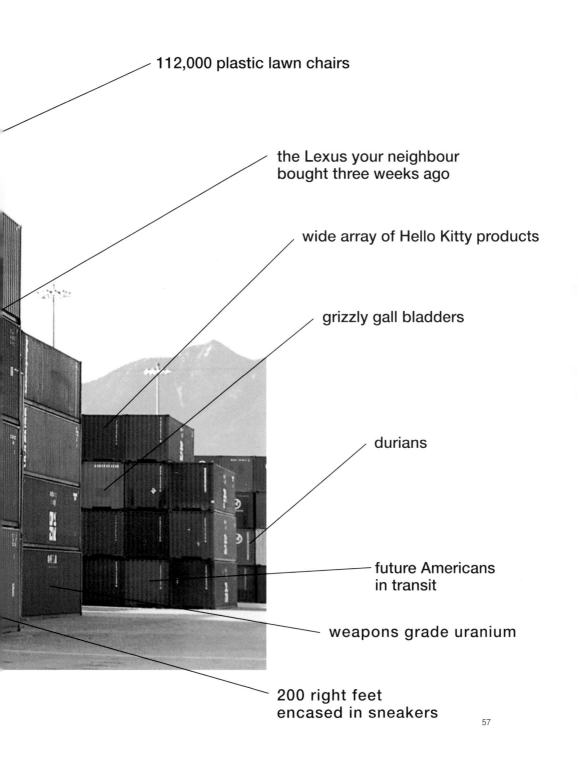

112,000 plastic lawn chairs

the Lexus your neighbour
bought three weeks ago

wide array of Hello Kitty products

grizzly gall bladders

durians

future Americans
in transit

weapons grade uranium

200 right feet
encased in sneakers

Highway 99...

... Highway of Doom. No, it really is. And yes, it's beautiful, sure—North America's southernmost fjord with endless (no pun intended) killer scenery—but this thing is a 300-kilometre (175-mile) ribbon of pain. It stretches from Horseshoe Bay up to Whistler and beyond into the depths of the Coastal Range—and it transforms humdrum human beings into fuming raging beasts with astonishing speed and consistency.

Basically, it was designed to carry a fraction of the cars it does now. It twists and hairpins and can go on forever without a passing lane, thus igniting the ire of drivers trapped behind logging trucks, trailer rigs and dawdling tourists who turn the fifty cars behind them into hostages as they cluelessly meander and drift through the mountain splendour. Locally, these clusters of hostages are called the "Snake" and on Sundays, the "Snake" headed into Vancouver from Whistler is 80 kilometres (50 miles) long. "Snakes" are dangerous because people do crazy insane stupid things when they're stuck in one. They pass on blind curves, they get stuck in one-on-one road rage wars with other drivers, and they drive at speeds that can only guarantee certain death when a Safeway super-trailer drives around the corner from the other direction.

Counterintuitively, the deadliest of Highway 99's accidents don't occur on twisty bits in the middle of rainy nights—they occur on the straightaway portions in the middle of the day when sunlight and the illusion of a safe passing stretch lure drivers to head-on deaths. The long, straight stretch at Furry Creek is the deadliest stretch of all.

And then there are rock slides. And then there are creeks overflowing from storms sending millions of litres of muddy cake batter down the near vertical slopes, absorbing whatever lies in the way. In 1925, one washout killed thirty-seven people and wiped out an entire town.

Officials like to say, "It's the people, not the road," but the fact is, it's the road. Be wary.

Kits

Whenever you see a beer commercial and wonder where all those beautiful, athletic, fun-loving, Jeep-driving beer drinkers live, the answer is that they live in Kitsilano, or "Kits." Kits is a residential area that looks across English Bay to the North Shore. *Volleyball! Sand! Tans! Dogs wearing scarves on their necks!* It's all there, and in summer it can be a real pick-me-up to see so many toned citizens volleyballing and Frisbee tossing. Kits is so perky that it almost begs the question, "Does it have a dark side to it?" The answer to this may well be, no, which is, in itself, a kind of darkness. Also, a bit further down the way from Kits is Jericho Beach, which is worth a visit in any kind of weather and offers some amazing panorama views of the city.

My Hotel Year

Part One: Cathy

It was some years ago. I had been going through a patch of intense brooding and had made a big hubbub about severing my ties to my past. I had moved into a rent-by-the-week cold water downtown hotel room on Granville Street and had cut all my hair off, stopped shaving and had thorns tattooed on my right arm. I spent my days lying on my bed staring at the ceiling, listening to the drunken brawls in other rooms, the squawk of other peoples' TVs and the smashing of furniture. My fellow tenants were a mixture of pensioners, runaways, drug dealers and so forth. The whole ensemble had made a suitably glamorous backdrop for my belief that my poverty, my fear of death, my sexual frustration and my inability to connect with others would carry me off into some sort of epiphany. I had lots of love to give—it's just that no one was taking it then. I had thought I was finding consolation in solitude, but to be honest I think I was only acquiring a veneer of bitterness.

My neighbours across the hall at this time were a headbanger couple, Cathy and Pup-Tent. Cathy was a runaway from Kamloops up north. Pup-Tent was a bit older and from back East. They both had the ghostly complexions, big hair and black leather wardrobe that heavy metal people like so much. They tended to live at night, and sleep late into the afternoon, but sometimes I'd see Pup-Tent being the very picture of enterprise down on Granville Street, selling hashish cut with Tender Vittles to treeplanters on city leave. Or I'd see Cathy, selling feather earrings in the rain on Robson Street. Sometimes I'd see them both at the corner grocery store where they'd be shopping for Kraft dinner, grenadine syrup, peeled carrot sticks, Cap'n Crunch, After Eight dinner mints and Lectric Shave. We'd nod in a neighbourly way, and occasionally we'd meet in the pub at the Yale Hotel and get to talking. It was via these encounters that I got to know them. They'd sit there drawing skulls and crossbones on each other's transdermal nicotine patches and drink draft beers.

Pup-Tent:	You want to talk?
Cathy:	No.
Pup-Tent:	Okay then.
	...a pause
Cathy:	Stop ignoring me.

By themselves they could be interesting, but as a twosome their conversation was a bit limited. Sometimes it's nice to sit with people and not say much of anything.

But any adoration in their relationship was strictly one-way. Cathy was in love with Pup-Tent—her first love—whereas I suspect Pup-Tent saw Cathy as just an interchangeable girlfriend unit. He'd "keep her in line" by flaunting the ease with which he could seduce other women. He was good looking by any standard, and his main pick-up technique was to pump out negative signals so that women with low self-esteem would be glued to him. In this way he could have the upper hand. A not-so-fresh barfly would ask him, "How old do you think I am, cutie?" and Pup-Tent would reply, "Thirty-three and divorced—or twenty-eight with a drinking problem." If she was his type, she'd be hooked then and there.

This flirting drove Cathy crazy. Sometimes when Pup-Tent disappeared from the table she'd tell me as much. When Cathy's sister, Donna, came down from Kamloops to visit her one day, she asked Cathy what it was she saw in Pup-Tent. "Let me get this straight, Cath: jail record ...violent ... no job....."

"Oh," said Cathy, "But I like the way he *walks*."

On evenings when Pup-Tent and I were by ourselves at the pub, he'd ask me things as, "How come a woman screwed up on drugs is so much scarier than a guy screwed up on drugs?" I'd reply, "Is this a joke?" And he'd say, "No. I'm seriously asking you."

In general, they seemed affable enough with each other, and most of the time their conversation moved along predictable lines:

Pup-Tent:	"Why are you staring at me?"
Cathy:	"I'm wondering what you're thinking about."
Pup-Tent:	"Why do you care about what I think?"
Cathy:	"Okay, I don't."
Pup-Tent:	"Then prove it by minding your own business."

After a while, though, the two of them began having fights that were loud enough to wake me from across the hall. Cathy would appear on the street with the occasional bruise or red eyeball. But as with most couples involved in this sort of relationship, the subject of domestic violence never came up in their conversations with others.
One day Cathy, myself and a street kid—a male exotic dancer on his day off—were discussing death over a plate of fries with gravy at Tat's Coffee Inn. The question was, "What do you think dying is like?" Cathy said it was like you're in a store, and a friend drives up to the door in a beautiful car and says, "Hop in—let's go for a trip!" And so off you go on a spin. And once you're on the road and having a great time, suddenly your friend turns to you to say, "Oh, by the way, you're dead," and you realize it's true, but it doesn't matter because you're happy, this is an adventure and this is fine.

Once, on a morning after a particularly noisy night, Cathy and I were down on Drake Street and we saw a crow standing in a puddle, motionless, the sky reflected on its surface so that the crow was standing on the sky. Cathy then told me that she thinks that there's a secret world just underneath the surface of our own world. She said that the secret world was more important than the one we live in. "Just imagine how surprised fish would be," she said, "if they knew about all the action going on just on the other side of the water. Or just imagine yourself being able to breathe underwater and living with the fish. The secret world is just like that and it's *that* different."

I said that the secret world reminded me of the world of sleep where time and gravity and things like that don't matter. She said that maybe they were both the same thing.

One day I came home from the library, where I had spent the afternoon trying to make people feel middle class by scowling at them. The door to Cathy and Pup-Tent's apartment was wide open, so I poked my head in and said "Hello?" I couldn't believe what a dump their place was—strewn with rusting bike chains, yellowed house plants, cigarette boxes and butts, Metallica blankets and Cathy's clothes. I said, "Cath? Pup? You guys in?" but there was no answer.

I stood there looking around when Cathy came in the door looking in awful condition and carrying a bag of Burger King food. She said that Pup-Tent was gone, that he'd taken off with a stripper to Vancouver Island and that, in the end, he had gone nuts because Cathy had erased all of his cassette tapes by microwaving them in his mini-microwave.

"I must look pretty bad, huh?"

"No," I said, "not at all."

"You hungry? Want some food?"

"Maybe later."

We stood in silence for a little while. Cathy picked up a few stray garments. Then she said, "You used to live up on the mountain, didn't you—over on the North Shore?"

I confirmed that I had grown up there.

"That's where the big lake is, right? The reservoir?"

I told her this was true.

"Then I need you to help me with something. What are you doing this afternoon?"

I replied, what am I *ever* doing in the afternoons?

Cathy wanted to see the reservoir up the Capilano Canyon, up behind Cleveland Dam. She wouldn't tell me why until we got there, but she seemed in an obviously unhappy state. Playing tour guide was the least I could do to cheer her up. And so we took the bus over to the North Shore, to the mountains overlooking the city.

The bus climbed up Capilano Road, past the suburban houses nested inside the tall Douglas firs, hemlocks and cedars. These houses seemed as far away from my then-life as to seem like China. Further up the mountain, the late afternoon sky was cloudy and dark. When the wet air of the Pacific Ocean hits the mountains, it dumps all of its wetness right there. The sky was just starting to rain as we got off the bus near Cleveland Dam and, as we crossed the road, I could tell we were going to get soaked.

The reservoir itself was a short walk away and was quickly enough pointed out to Cathy, but she looked disappointed when she saw it, though—the large loch-like lake stretching back into the deep dark mountain valley. She said, "Like, what's with the barbed wire fence? You mean we can't go in and touch the water?"

"I said we couldn't, not from where we were.

"You mean we have another option?"

I said we did, but it would involve some tromping through the woods, and she said this was just fine, and so we headed up the road past a sign saying: WATERSHED: NO ADMITTANCE to a place where we used to have outdoor parties when I was in high school.

Cathy sullenly smoked a cigarette and clutched her purse to her side as we walked past the gate and up the dirt access road. The mountains above us were cloaked in mist up at their tops and we heard only an occasional bird noise as we cut off the road and into the trees. Cathy was immediately drenched as we cut through the underbrush of salmonberry bushes, grasses and juvenile firs. Her big hair was filled with spider-webs and fir needles and dead huckleberry leaves; her black jeans were wet and clammy at her ankles. I asked her if she wanted to go back, but she said, no, we had to continue, and so we did, tromping deep into the black echo-free woods until we saw the glint of water ahead of us—the reservoir. Cathy then said to me, "Stop—don't move," and I froze.

I thought she'd seen a bear or had pulled a gun out of her purse. I turned around and she had frozen in mid-motion. She said, "I bet if we froze right here, and didn't move and didn't breathe, we could stop time."

And so we stood there, deep in the woods, frozen in motion, trying to stop time.

Now: I believed that you've had most of your important memories by the time you're thirty. After that, memory becomes water overflowing into an already full cup. New experiences just don't register in the same way or with the same impact. I could be shooting heroin with the Princess of Wales, naked in a crashing jet, and the experience still couldn't compare to the time the cops chased us after we threw the Taylor's patio furniture into their pool in the eleventh grade. You know what I mean.

I think that Cathy at some level felt this way, too—and that she realized that all of her important memories would soon enough be taken—that she had X-number of years ahead of her of falling for the wrong guys—mistreaters and abusers—and that all of her memory would then be used up in sadness and dead ends and in being hurt, and at the end of it all would be … nothing—no more new feelings.

Sometimes I think the people to feel the saddest for are people who are unable to connect with the profound—people such as my boring brother-in-law, a hearty type so concerned with normality and fitting in that he eliminates any possibility of uniqueness for himself and his own personality. I wonder if some day, when he's older, he'll wake up and that deeper part of him will realize that he's never allowed himself to truly exist, and he'll cry with regret and shame and grief.

And then sometimes I think the people to feel saddest for are people who once knew what profoundness was, but who lost or became numb to the sensation of wonder—people who closed the doors that lead us into the secret world—or who had the doors closed for them by time and neglect and decisions made in times of weakness.

What happened was this: Cathy and I walked to the edge of the reservoir, and from her purse she removed a Ziploc baggie containing two rather stupid-looking goldfish that Pup-Tent had bought for her the week before in an isolated moment of kindness. We sat down on the smooth rocks next to the spotless, clean, infinitely dark and deep lake water. She said to me, "You only get one chance to fall in love for the first time, don't you?"

And I said, "Well, at least you got the chance. A lot of people are still waiting."

She then poked into the glassy still water, made small ripples and threw a stone or two. Then she took the baggie, placed it under the water and punctured the membrane with her sharp black fingernails. "Bye-bye, fishies," she said as they languidly wriggled down into the depths. "Make sure you two stay together. You're the only chance that either of you is ever going to get."

Part 2: Donny

Donny was a hustler who lived at the end of the hall in the tiny room next to the bathroom. He was young and friendly, and sometimes would ask me to have dinner with him, but dinner usually turned out to be blue Popsicles, Velveeta cheese and beer in his dingy room where the paint peeled and you could see how many colours the room had been before. The only technology in the room was a phone answering machine he used to reply to ads he placed in the paper. I'd feel sorry for him. Even though I was broke I'd find a way to treat him to dinner at the A&W.

Donny would do anything with anybody, but mostly, he said, people didn't want to do much. A sixteen-year-old girl asked him to sit in a hot tub with her with no clothes; an older, yuppie-type businesswoman paid him $250.00 just to go see *Batman Returns* with her.

Every afternoon around dark, when the windows got dark enough to turn into mirrors, Donny would come out of the bathroom with wet short black hair which he'd shake like a dog, and then tramp down the hotel's creaky old stairs and pursue the evening's commerce. He said he thought of himself as an entrepreneur; he said the guys on the street had given him a nickname: Púttáno, Boy Slut. He said anything was better than the job he had before, driving a shuttle bus between the airport and one of the downtown hotels.

Donny was always getting stabbed. His skin was beginning to look
like an old leather couch at the Greyhound station, but this didn't
bother him at all. One night after a flare up on the sidewalk after an
Alexis-versus-Krystal drag night at one of the clubs, Donny came
home with a half dozen calligraphic red slashes all over his stomach.
I tried to make him go to St. Paul's for stitches but he wouldn't.
When I asked him if he was worried about permanent damage he
gave me a guarded look and said, "This is my life and this is how I
live it." I never hassled him after that.

But Donny actively invited stabbing into his life. He said that
being stabbed didn't hurt nearly as much as you'd think, and that it
was actually kind of cool, and that when it happened, "Man, when
that blade first digs into you it makes your soul leap out of your
body for just a second, like a salmon jumping out of a river."

I do remember him telling me, though, that he was actually
getting a little bored of being stabbed. He said that in the end his big
goal was to get shot. He was so curious to know what being shot
would be like. To facilitate shooting he would always wear his
shirts wide open at the chest, like a 1976 person.

Donny showed up nearer the end of my stay at the hotel—a period when I was wondering if I would eventually be exhausted by the effort it was taking to cope with solitude.

I think it takes an amazing amount of energy just to convince oneself that the Forever Person isn't just around the next corner. In the end I believe we never do convince ourselves. I know that I found it increasingly hard to maintain the pose of emotional self-sufficiency lying on my bed and sitting at my desk, watching the seagulls cartwheeling over the bridges, cradling myself in my own arms, breathing warm chocolate-and-vodka breath on a rose I'd found on a streetcorner, trying to force it to bloom.

Time ticks by; we grow older. Before we know it, too much time has passed and we've missed the chance to have had other people hurt us. To a younger me, this sounded like luck; to an older me, this sounds like a quiet tragedy.

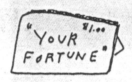

Sometimes Donny and Cathy and me would walk the streets together on a sunny day and just bum around. The innocence of this activity made our lives seem a bit less dark. We'd buy ice creams, Donny would walk on his hands, and we'd all play "mock the stock" at some of the more exotic bondage and sex stores.

Once in the early evening we walked past a fortune teller— a grizzled old soak sitting forlornly behind a card table on which rested a Japanese paper carp with a burning candle inside. In his hands he clutched a deck of tarot cards probably salvaged from a dumpster. We kidded Donny and said he should have his fortune read, but he freaked and refused flat out. "I'm not having some old rubby tell me my future. Man, he probably lives in an old fridge under the Burrard Bridge. He probably sits in his fridge and molests tennis starlets all day."

We didn't press the issue, and if the fortune teller heard Donny's comments, he gave no indication and we walked on.

It was only a few weeks later that I saw Donny, cheerfully being told his fortune by the same old fortune teller. I walked up to him and said, "Hey, Sport—I thought you didn't want to have your fortune told to you."

And Donny very matter-of-factly said, "Hey, guy—didn't you see the sign here?" He pointed to some words lopsidedly felt-penned on a sheet of packing cardboard next to the candle which read:

I PROMiSS I wonT TeLL You YOuR gOING TO DIE.

"That's all it takes, Man. It's all I ever wanted to hear. Keep on reading, Mister."

This is not a long story. In the end Donny got his wish, and he did get shot—over a very stupid drug deal that imploded in a Chinatown parking lot—twice in the back of the head and once in the back. I ended up having to identify the body as nobody knew where his family was or who they even were. I guess his salmon jumped out of the river and onto land, and the river itself flows on.

I left the hotel shortly thereafter and, very soon after that, I fell in love. Love was frightening and it hurt—not only during, but afterward—when I fell out of love. But that is another story.

I'd like to fall in love again but my only hope is that love doesn't happen to me so often after this. I don't want to get so used to falling in love that I get curious to experience something more extreme—whatever that may be.

end

Love Boats

From April until September, glistening white Love Boats glide in and out of the city's harbour, their rosters consisting mostly of American couples curious to see the northern glaciers calve and to watch the carved ice swans melt amid the never-ending buffet meal that is the cruise-liner lifestyle. There used to be only a few liners every year, but now there are several a day. Why? Marketing surveys showing that while Seattle might well be logistically and technically a better place for passengers to board the ships, Vancouver is perceived as being "more exotic"—an unexpected bonus of Canada's 1970 conversion to metric road signs.

In the late afternoon, the liners—gargantuan, imperious and white—sail out from under Lions Gate Bridge in a clean, confident flotilla. This parade can only trigger in spectators thoughts of the afterlife, watching a collection of souls headed off to a cleaner, purer place. The dark side of cruise ships? The Norwalk virus and mid-sea sewage dumps from all those folks eating seventeen meals a day. And a recent U.S. study found that cruise ships are the second-most dangerous place to be outside of active war zones.

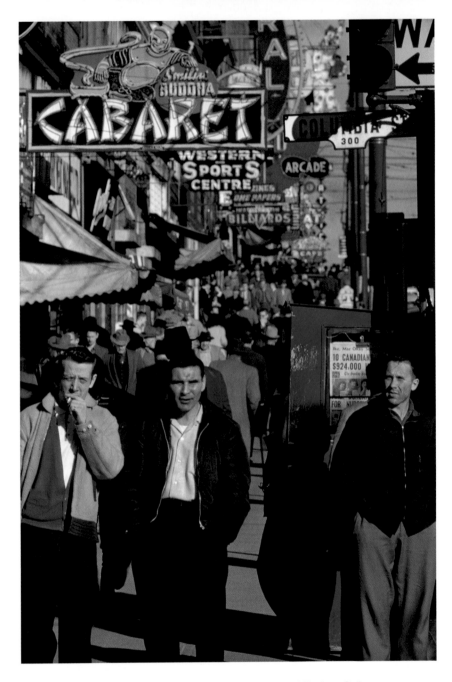

Fred Herzog, *Hastings at Columbia,* 1958, courtesy of Equinox Gallery

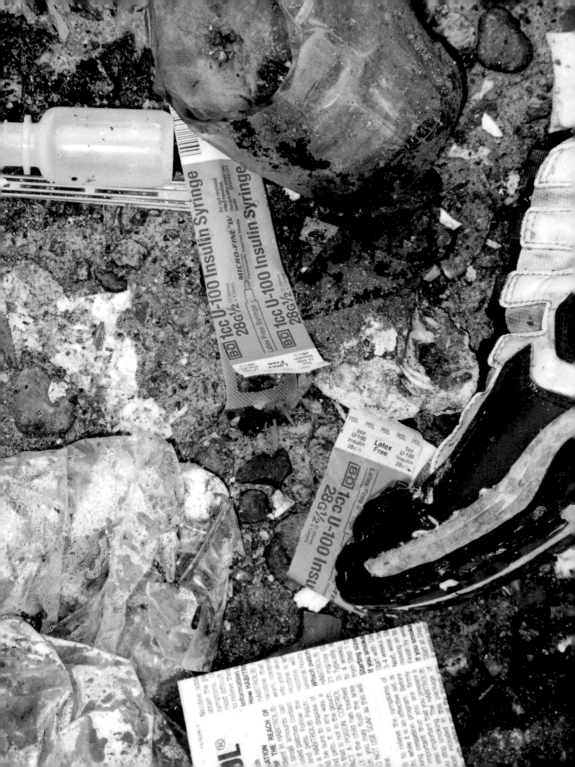

Main & Hastings

Vancouver's a port city. Heroin is a given. The corner of Main and Hastings is in the poorest postal code in Canada and is home to untold social ills, not the least of which is smack. Adding to its weirdness is its close proximity to perky, cruise-liner friendly Gastown and to fastidious Chinatown.

This is a part of the city that is in chronic pain. The alleys feature snowdrifts of syringes, bleach bottles, alcohol swab wrappers, orange syringe tips and tiny plastic bags used to hold crack crystals. The amount of drug paraphernalia littering the place is astounding. You expect maybe a syringe or two and you see ... hundreds. Also very common are empty cans of meal replacement products such as Boost and Ensure—relatively fast, cheap ways of getting bare-bones nutrition. Interestingly, cigarette butts are few; money spent on cigarettes is money that could have been spent on drugs.

I lived for years at the corner of Powell and Columbia, the northwest corner of the district, and have many happy memories of the place, but I pretty much avoided the alleys, and the streets can get deeply ugly after 2:00 A.M. when the bars close, or on Welfare Wednesday when the cheques get cashed and the social wreckage stacks up.

Having said all of this, it's a place one ought to see and not particularly fear. It's disturbing and intense, but the place is populated by people with souls just like anybody else. Wear sturdy footwear, lock the car, and open your mind and your eyes.

Okay, it's a gross picture, but it's a common one, too. The small white bottles contain bleach used for cleaning out reused needles.

Monster Houses

In the 1980s, a very (then) strange type of house began popping up all over Vancouver. They were huge—vast—most often stuccoed, had very few outdoor details and were skimpy to the point of sterility when it came to trees and gardens. They made about as much sense in the neighbourhoods into which they were inserted as a UFO in Versailles. They were awkward, frequently designed in the worst postmodern style and weren't at all concerned about their communities. With all objectivity, they could at best be described as ... homely. These became locally known as "monster houses."

These houses still remain, but many are now hidden behind tall cedar hedges; new monster houses aren't being built, as the trend now is toward the Arts & Crafts/ski-lodge style, "The Whistler Style," which can be equally monstrous if done improperly, but at least it makes an effort at integrating with the surroundings and history.

I once wrote a piece about monster houses in the Brentwood section of Los Angeles that I think applies equally to Vancouver:

> The monsters we create as a culture at any one time reflect our deepest collective terrors sublimated through a single entity. In the 1950s our monsters were pod people. In the 1960s, monsters were googly-eyed, Rat Fink, Revell model chummy things, anonymously designed folkloric terror, and lovable at the core: Incredible Edibles, Wacky Packs, Herman Munster. In the 1970s we had Jaws. But what is our vision of monsters now? There no longer seems to be friendliness attached to them; they are now merely out to kill (just visit any video rental shop), or they're out to—*shiver*—devalue our neighbourhoods.

My own neighbourhood got monstered over the past decade. My authentic and quiet suburban street has been transformed into a Disney version of what an authentic and quiet suburban street ought to be. It makes the land more valuable, yes, but it's not really land any more. It's something else— a real estate brochure and not a neighbourhood. But these things are scary—and that's what monsters do.

Photo by Arni Haraldsson, *Canterbury Place, Phase II,* British Properties, West Vancouver, BC, 1994

Mt. Baker

Off to the east, about 100 kilometres (60 miles) away from downtown, lies Mount Baker, an American Fuji, the most northerly of the necklace of American coastal volcanoes that, from north to south are:

Mount Baker
Mount Rainier
Mount Adams
Mount St. Helens
Mount Hood
Three Sisters
Mount Mazama (home of Crater Lake)
Mount Shasta
Lassen Peak

Interesting fact: in the twelve-month calendar period spanning July 1998 to July 1999, Mount Baker set the all-time planetary record for the Most Snow Ever to Fall—2896 centimetres (1,140 inches). Yes, you read that correctly—the all-time planetary record.

Mount Baker is important to the Vancouver psyche in that it stands there, huge, record-breaking and serene, shooting off just enough steam every few years to let us know that if it really wanted to, it could bury us. It's a metaphor for the United States: seductive but distant, powerful and at least temporarily benign.

Left   Photo by Robert Linsley, detail *Winter Sports,* New Westminster, #19 from *One Hundred Views of Mt Baker,* 1997.

North Shore Mountain Biking

The three mountains that backstop the City and District of North Vancouver and the "Special Municipal Prosperity Zone" of West Vancouver are better-known by their ski-area brand names: Cypress, Grouse and Seymour. Skiing and snowboarding are the most visible activities: with blankets of snow, it's easy to see the ski runs that are cut out of the forest, and the night skiing lights that adorn the lift towers are the jewels in the Triple Crown.

But in the steep evergreen rainforest between the hard-stop of suburbia and the snowline, out of sight and out of mind, it is the sport of freeride mountain biking that has progressed farther and faster than anywhere else in the world. Stand and watch by the yellow gate at the top of Mountain Highway, the foot of the Cypress or Mt Seymour Parkway, or the end of Riverside Drive, and you will be amazed at the number of mud-splattered riders in full-face helmets and body armour that pour out of the trail heads. Straddling fully suspended Vancouver-designed and Shore-tested bikes by Rocky Mountain, Banshee, Kona, Norco or Cove (as in Deep Cove), they'll home in on pickup trucks that are often worth less than the bikes they load in the back and shuttle back up for another descent. You won't know these riders' names, like you might know the skateboarder Tony Hawk, but when Red Bull hosts a freeride contest somewhere in the U.S. or Europe, it's not unusual for half of the top-ten finishers to be from Vancouver and the Shore.

So why here? With apologies to Richard Florida, there is no "xTR3M3 Ind-X" or other magic formula that can be templated and repeated elsewhere. Vancouver and the North Shore represent a large metropolitan area with shockingly easy access to extreme terrain and conditions. That's obvious, and there are other cities —Salt Lake, Honolulu—that offer similar proximity and access. But the kind of explosion in skills and technology requires a catalyst, and in the case of freeriding, it's provided by that most endemic of natural materials, fallen cedar. For the same reasons that the First Nations of the Northwest Coast used it for building (it splits easily, is durable and rot-resistant and is everywhere), riders and trail builders found they could improve the flow of a descent by making ramps and bridges over logs and marshes. What a few of us started doing in the early 1980s with a few rotten logs has evolved into an Ewok Village of increasingly complex constructions on trails with evocative names like Boogieman, Pink Starfish, Air Supply, Pipeline, The Circus, Coiler and Seventh Secret.

Evolution is accelerated in harsh, isolated ecologies, and like the finches of the Galapagos Islands, a Shore rider is a unique species. The price of failure is high: it's one thing to wipe out in the surf or on snow, it's quite another to fall from a 30-centimetre (12-inch) wide log ride that's 6 metres (20 feet) above rocks and trees. If you go looking for these trails, you won't get directions from the locals. Don't take it personally; they are trying to protect you from getting seriously hurt. As the saying goes, when the rider is ready, the trail will reveal itself.

Number 8

The number 8 is good luck in Chinese culture. In the late 1990s, when there was uncertainty about Hong Kong's future, Vancouver condo tower builders fell all over themselves trying to get their buildings assigned addresses containing lots and lots of 8's, a move that was a little bit embarrassing to watch at the time (1888 Pacific, 888 Pacific etc.). But after a while, it became a habit to slap an 8 onto everything, and now you see 8's just about everywhere. If in doubt, check out the phone numbers of real estate agents and moving companies.

When I went to get a new cellphone number last year, the local provider, Telus, asked if I wanted the "Asian Option." I said yes, so the guy clicked onto the onscreen box and I received a new number with four eights in it.

The bad-luck number you *don't* want to use is 4. If your address is 444 44th Street, it's like living at 666 Slow-Drawn-Out Death Street. The number 7 is unlucky too, but 4 is definitely the worst. The place where you really see this in operation is in Vancouver elevators, which are possibly unique in the world in that their keypads lack floors numbered 4, 13, 14, 24, 34 and 44.

ELEVATOR 3
907 KG

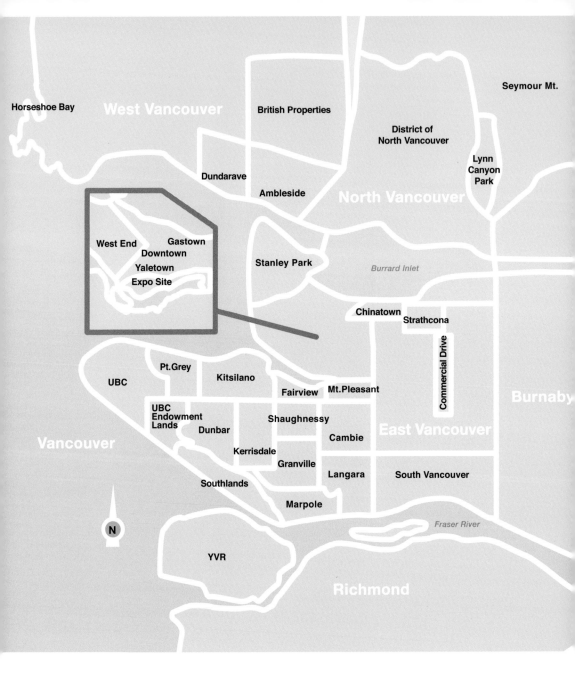

Horseshoe Bay

West Vancouver

British Properties

Seymour Mt.

District of
North Vancouver

Lynn
Canyon
Park

Dundarave

Ambleside

North Vancouver

West End

Gastown

Downtown

Yaletown

Expo Site

Stanley Park

Burrard Inlet

Chinatown

Strathcona

Commercial Drive

Pt.Grey

Kitsilano

UBC

Fairview

Mt.Pleasant

Burnaby

UBC
Endowment
Lands

Dunbar

Shaughnessy

Vancouver

Kerrisdale

Cambie

East Vancouver

Granville

Southlands

Langara

South Vancouver

Marpole

Fraser River

N

YVR

Richmond

Vancouver

Parallel Universe Vancouver

Post & Beam

Vancouver has a few really good buildings and a few kind of okay buildings, but mostly it's a city of (and it really depresses me to say this) indifferent and terrible buildings. The bad buildings are no accident. If Paris is a city of monuments, and if Tokyo is a city of small beautiful moments, Vancouver is a city of scenery. It coasts on its scenery quite shamelessly, and many builders take advantage of our love of mountain views to build charmless concrete dumps—and when you call them on it, they say, "Oh, but I didn't want to draw attention away from the beautiful view." Yeah, right. Many Vancouverites carry around mental detonators and, as they walk around the city, eliminate eyesore after eyesore. My nominee is Park Royal Mall in West Vancouver, but that's just me. Everybody's hit list is different.

Architecture in Vancouver wasn't always so awful. In fact, in the three decades following WW2, the world looked to Vancouver for innovation and creativity. The dominant style of the era, pioneered in Vancouver and exported around the world, is called "post & beam." One of this style's main attributes is the (then) radical flat roof, as well as large windows that merge the interior of the home with the exterior, a possible metaphor for the Vancouverite's psyche as well.

The post & beam house is not a rancher. Ranchers are fine, but their roots are Californian, and they were created simply for relaxed carefree living. The post & beam house, though, was designed to spur on the modernist idea of a better human society through better design, and not just in a lots-of-fresh-air-and-exercise manner. The simplicity and lack of pretense was meant to imbue inhabitants with an appreciation for simpler, more natural and progressive ideas. That's a lot for a building to do. Curiously, most of these houses, given a coat of paint and a few good pieces of furniture, could easily fit into any current architectural magazine with ease—they *work*.

Many factors converged to make Vancouver such an innovative postwar architectural hot spot: the forest industry's need to create demand for plywood, the need for more family housing, and the often dramatic and challenging vertical landscapes of West Van and North Van. Canadian style magazines from 1950 to 1965 might just as well have dubbed it "North Shore Architecture."

In the 1970s Vancouver's dominant style became a sort of cedar brutalism,

best typified in the era's ski and alpine structures: 45-degree angles were all the rage—and supergraphics, bold clean bands of colour taking us around our walls and into our future. In the '80s and '90s came monster houses, but that's another category altogether. Now, in the first millennial decade, the official style of architecture is "ski lodge," a taste perfected during the explosive growth of Whistler in the 1990s: lots of eaves and river rock and shingled walls. There is hope on the horizon: many builders have realized that nothing guarantees resale value more than good design. Finally!

Real Estate!

Real estate gets an exclamation mark because it's Vancouver's biggest sport, way ahead of skiing and sailing, and is disturbingly central to the civic psyche. Real estate agents are local celebs of sorts, and the weekly homes section of the paper is scrutinized like a fortune cookie. Those people who own property resemble Microsoft employees who check their computers every few hours to see their net worth go up ... or down. Recent fluctuations have just made the sport even bloodier and more compelling. No other real estate market in North America is as dependent on the ups and downs of Asian politics or on simply having a place to sit and watch a nice sunset.

The health of a neighbourhood is indicated by the number of "FOR SALE" signs out front: too few is bad but too many is very, very, very bad. One "FOR SALE" sign per block is what you want. For the price of a one-bedroom Kleenex box in Vancouver, you can buy a five-bedroom stone house with an acre of land anywhere else in Canada.

If the conversation is ever lulling with a Vancouverite, bring up the subject of real estate and sit back to watch the conversation go on autopilot. And for anybody who's ever tried renting anything halfway decent in Vancouver, the only way to pay the rent is to start a marijuana grow-op.

```
0100    ??  ?? ????      ??:??  ??:??  C??      ????
.30         Toronto        14:30  14:30  C46
7315        Williams Lake  14:35  14:35  B19
296         Winnipeg       14:35  14:35  C51
4748        Montreal       14:40  14:40  C44
4748        Montreal       14:40  14:40  C44
7349        Comox          14:50  14:50  B19
8194        Kamloops       14:55  14:55  C34C
218         Calgary        15:00  15:00  B16
9592        Victoria       15:00  15:00  C34B
9592        Victoria       15:00  15:00  C34B
8416        Kelowna        15:30  15:30  C47
244         Edmonton       15:40  15:40  B15
220         Calgary        16:00  16:00  B12
8073        Victoria       16:00  16:00  C34F
8352        Penticton      16:05  16:05  C34G
7347        Campbell Rv    16:10  16:10  B19
152         Toronto        16:15  16:15  C46
188         Ottawa         16:25  16:25  C44
```

The Rest of Canada

Vancouver is not part of Canada. Not really. There's a genuine sense of disconnection from the Rest of Canada that we feel here. While Ontario looms large in the minds of most other Canadians, said province simply doesn't enter our minds from one week to the next.

In looking through the souvenir book from my high school's twentieth-year reunion (Sentinel Class of 1979), I noticed that dozens and dozens of classmates had married Americans from Washington, Oregon and California, and only a small number had connected in any way to the east. This makes sense; Vancouverites have much in common with West Coast Americans, and at the same time remain highly distinct from them. Americans wonder how Vancouverites can be so cavalier about their link to Canada, so you have to tell

AC8282	Prince Rupert	17:00	17:00	C34B	
AC8075	Victoria	17:00	17:00	C34E	
AC8324	Calgary	17:15	17:15	B11	
AC8576	Saskatoon	17:15	17:15	B15	
AC8244	Terrace	17:15	17:15	C34D	
AC8215	Cranbrook	17:30	17:30	C34G	
AC8265	Nanaimo	17:30	17:30	C34J	
AC8418	Kelowna	17:35	17:35	B18	
AC246	Edmonton	17:40	17:40	B12	
AC132	Toronto	17:40	23:50	B22	Tard
AC8562	Smithers	17:40	17:40	C34C	
AC8077	Victoria	18:00	18:00	C34F	
AC7309	Williams_Lake	18:15	18:15	B19	
AC8185	Ft St John	18:25	18:25	C34E	
AC8196	Kamloops	18:30	18:30	C34B	
AC8209	Prince George	18:45	18:45	C31	
LH9643	Calgary	18:55	18:55	B11	
LH9643	Calgary	18:55	18:55	B11	

them that, every decade or so, votes are held back east to see if the country even plans to stick together.

There's nothing unpatriotic about Vancouver's psychic disconnection from the Rest of Canada—it's a reality fostered by Vancouver's distance from Canada's centre and from a tradition of abandoning that very centre to try something new. To ignore these factors would be foolish. In a thousand years, Canada won't be the same country it is now, nor will it probably be the same in five hundred, a hundred, fifty or even ten. My own hunch is that Vancouver will eventually evolve into a city state going as far north as Whistler, as far east as the Fraser Canyon and then to the U.S. border.

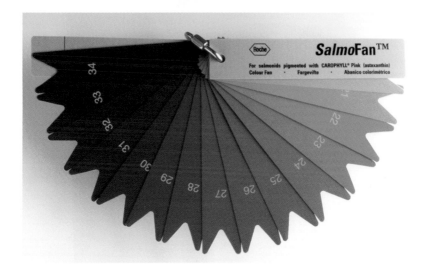

Salmon

Salmon is a big deal in Vancouver. It's pretty much our official fish, and anyone who's entered the gravitational warp of souvenir shops is well aware of its abundance in smoked form.

Up the Capilano River in North Vancouver is a fish hatchery. It's near my old elementary school, and as youngsters, we were dragged there on field trips usually twice a year by teachers who thought they were the first to ever have the idea. In autumn, the hatchery is an awesome sight as thousands of salmon return home to have sex and die. It's primal.

Once, an old art school friend, Rick, came to Vancouver from Berlin, where he'd been living a highly metropolitan life for some years. He wanted to see some hardcore nature, "but somewhere easy to drive from downtown," so I took him to the Capilano Canyon, fifteen minutes away.

Tourist season was over, and we essentially had the park to ourselves. We walked through the forest on either side of the canyon and, near the end of the walk, we went right down to the river shallows, maybe a few hundred metres from the entrance to the fish hatchery. The river was deadly still—the Cleveland Dam, the reservoir that feeds the Capilano, had essentially turned off the water; the river was a series of motionless pools.

In one of these pools was a school of salmon, which had turned purple and red as they neared the end of their life cycle. There were perhaps a thousand of them all clustered together in a clump the shape of a brain, stable, swimming in one place. It was one of the most beautiful sights I'd ever seen. On an impulse, I stripped down to my BVDs and stepped into the water, cold to say the least, and walked right into the middle of "the brain," with these creatures swimming around me. I tried to imagine what it is they could be thinking—some message so old and so basic that earthly newcomers like humans would never get it.

Do we get the message? Salmon stocks are dwindling, and nobody's quite sure why. This loss can sometimes feel as if there's a hole in the collective soul. I don't like eating salmon or salmon sashimi—I prefer raw tuna. But I know that salmon comes *from* here and that salmon partly defines us and has defined inhabitants for thousands of years—salmon was the first form of currency used by First Nations people. I think that most Vancouverites at some point throughout their week invariably sit back and quietly wonder what message it is we're being sent by living here, and it's more than just knowing we have to count our blessings. It's wondering about this one intangible unanswerable question that, possibly, more than any other thing, defines a person as a Vancouverite.

Seattle

Vancouverites commonly visit Seattle about once a year. You'd think two cities so close to each other, with similar populations and geography, would be alike, but you'd be wrong. Seattle sees itself as being a spit away from Alaska—they really ham up the Klondike connection big time. *"Oh my God! We just got word in from Skagway and it's going to be a raining tonight ... Arrrrrr!"* Seattleites like to think of themselves as resembling the guy on the Brawny paper towel label. Or Bill Gates.

On the other hand, Vancouver sees itself as the warmest place in Canada, a sort of colder, rainier Malibu. Vancouverites drive around with the top down in February and sit at outside bistros in March, activities that would be unthinkable three hours south in Seattle.

Vancouver also sees itself as the end of the line—if you live in Canada and you want to either reinvent yourself or enter your own witness relocation project, Vancouver is where you go. Seattle, in being the gateway to Alaska, by default forfeits its role as End of the Line.

Also, Seattle also actually makes *things*—747s and such—whereas Vancouver isn't really a thing-making place. Like simpletons, we ship away all our raw materials.

When Vancouverites think of Seattle, they think mostly about eighteen-lane gridlocked freeways that run in all directions, frequently with lanes stacked on top of each other. They also think of the huge mounds of food—vast heaving groaning portions of food—dished up at restaurants along I-5.

When Seattleites think of Vancouver (which is not as often as you might think—and many Americans who really ought to know better call Vancouver Island "Victoria Island"), they think of it as a weird city that has no freeways and where getting from anywhere to anywhere involves complex routes and many stoplights.

Both views of each other are correct.

One interesting new trend in Vancouver is that of Seattle tech firms such as Microsoft opening Canadian branch plants because the U.S. government is unwilling to grant visas to highly trained workers from other countries. Their loss, our gain.

Lions Gate

Perhaps in your city there is a structure so potent and glorious that its existence in your mind becomes the actual architecture of your mind—a structure through which all of your dreams and ideas and hopes are funnelled.

In my city, Vancouver, there is one such structure, a fairy-tale bridge called Lions Gate Bridge. Its three delicate spans link the city of Vancouver with the suburbs of the North Shore, where I grew up, and with the mountains and wilderness of British Columbia beyond those suburbs.

The only other road access to the North Shore is 8 kilometres (5 miles) down the harbour to the utilitarian and unfortunately rather charmless Second Narrows Bridge: a six-lane people-mover about which little more can be said without taxing the limits of charity.

* * *

Lions Gate Bridge is by no means a practical bridge—it looks to be spun from liquid sugar, and, unfortunately, it now seems to be dissolving like sugar. By urban planning and engineering standards it borders on being a disaster, but then isn't it true of life in general that nothing is more seductive than the dying starlet? The lost cowboy? The self-destructive jazz musician?

The bridge has three harrowingly narrow lanes. Depending on the time of day, commuters on the Lions Gate may have either one or two of these lanes apportioned to them. The rule of thumb is, tormentingly, the more traffic moving in your direction, the higher the probability of having only one lane.

* * *

But enough about the bridge's technicalities. We tolerate goodness knows how much from the people we love; the same goes for objects we love, too. I figure I have driven across the bridge maybe five or six thousand times in my life—that's all the way from Vancouver to Halifax and back—and never in all these miles have I once tired of the view, endlessly renewing, endlessly glorious.

Some of my happiest memories of Vancouver, or my life, for that matter, have been simple memories of driving across Lions Gate Bridge. In my mind, the AM radio is playing Heart's "Dreamboat Annie," the sulphur piles of North Vancouver shine their dim yellow hues, and the ocean and the boats and the mountains of West Vancouver shimmer like Tina Louise's gown.

Maybe I am headed to my parents' house or maybe I am off to the airport—the bridge's very existence is a metaphor for journey.

* * *

Like most regular Lions Gate Bridge drivers, I have my own little set of bridge quirks and observations. For example I get angry if I see a driver who discourteously breaks the one-two/one-two pattern of merging onto the north end: four lanes of traffic grudgingly, yet with decorum, braid into one.

Also, I have noticed that within moments of driving onto the bridge from the north end, most people instantly turn on their radios or stereos. I have no theory why they do this, but they just lunge for the dials.

As well, I have always noticed that traffic headed cityward mysteriously slows to a crawl once it hits the bridge's first draping span. It then shortly resumes its normal speed. I ascribe this predictable slowdown to people who are not from Vancouver. When they suddenly encounter the beauty that surrounds them from mid-bridge—the quartz of the city to the south; the freighters below, plump with wheat and ore; the cruise liners tramping away off in the distance; as well as the swoop of the bridge above them—the out-of-towners are overwhelmed. They respond by jamming on their brakes.

In an odd way this makes me proud of my city—proud to live here. I never begrudge this inevitable slowdown.

For people who don't normally drive Lions Gate Bridge, discussion of bridge traffic by regular drivers can seem endlessly bothersome and incomprehensible:

"How was bridge traffic?"

"One lane."

"Standstill?"

"Yup."

"Both lanes the other way empty?"

"Yup."

"Ferry must have come in at Horseshoe Bay."

"I was going to take the Second Narrows but I thought Lions Gate would be clear after seven P.M."

"Do ferries arrive on the odd hour or the even hour?"

"Oh, and there was a stall … "

(Insert scream from non-bridge driver here.)

* * *

A bridge memory.

One night in 1982, shortly after midnight when art school had closed, I was driving in my old rusted yellow VW Rabbit through the Stanley Park causeway that funnels into the bridge toward the North Shore. Suddenly, the traffic in my lane ground to a stop and traffic in the lanes from the other direction vanished altogether.

Something was up.

I turned off my ignition and walked a short way nearer the bridge's south approach, where I quickly learned, as did the other drivers who emerged from their cars (with little question marks inside the thought balloons above their heads), that there was "a jumper" up in the bridge's riggings.

Ooohhh …

I headed back to my car to wait out the drama. Shortly, though, I began to hear horn music playing, live music, not a stereo, and I walked down to the mouth of the bridge, where a bearded man in a white suit stood on the roof of a white Cadillac parked between the two cement lions guarding the entrance. He was serenading the jumper on the bridge with "Stranger on the Shore."

The man with the horn was Frank Baker, a restaurant owner of that long-vanished era when "fine dining" meant a T-bone steak, three double scotches and a pack of Chesterfields.

Mr. Baker, who died in 1991, had once owned a "swinging" kind of restaurant in West Vancouver where your parents would take out-of-town guests, but only after first getting themselves all revved up with Herb Alpert records.

Mr. Baker was always, to younger eyes, the embodiment of a certain type of cool, so cool that he had even bought the original Aston Martin DB-5 used in the James Bond movie *Goldfinger*. He was certainly a character, and his restaurant was an occupational puppy mill for a good number of friends during high school who bussed there and diced the vegetables and did food-prep on weekends.

But Frank Baker was also a good musician, and that night on the bridge people like myself sat in the grass and daffodils along the banks of the causeway and listened to his songs, wondering, I guess, if we too might ever reach that point in life when we would find ourselves in the riggings of Lions Gate Bridge, trying to decide yes? or no?, knowing that even if we decided yes, a water landing still offered a semblance of hope.

* * *

Another memory:

In late 1986 I arrived back in Vancouver after living abroad for a year. On that first evening back I looked down at the bridge and saw that it had been garlanded with brilliant pearls of light along its thin parabolic lines. I was shocked—it was so beautiful it made me lose my breath.

I asked my father about these lights, and he told me they were called "Gracie's Necklace," after a local politician. In the almost five decades since the bridge had been built, the city had been secretly dreaming of the day when it would cloak its bridge in light, and now the dream had become real life.

Now, whenever I fly back to Vancouver, it is Gracie's Necklace I look for from my seat, the sight I need to see in order to make myself feel I am home again. We often forget, living here in Vancouver, that we live in the youngest city on Earth, a city almost entirely of, and only of, the twentieth century—and that this is Vancouver's greatest blessing. It is the delicacy of Gracie's Necklace that reminds me we live, not so much in a city but in a dream of a city.

* * *

Now, I was not a particularly standout student in high school. I seem to remember spending the bulk of those years more or less catatonic from understimulation. One of the few respites from the school's daily underdosings of learning was the view from up the mountain of the bridge, the city, Mount Baker, of Vancouver Island and of the never-ending cranes continually transforming the skyline.

In October, the fogs would roll in; the city below became a glowing, foaming prairie of white light. Lions Gate Bridge would puncture through that light, glowing gold, offering transport into that other, luminous arena.

For grades 8, 9, 10 and most of grade 11, I spent many hours slumped over the physics class radiator, dreaming of the day—January 13, 1978—two weeks after my sixteenth birthday, when I would pass my driver's test and at last be able to drive into that magic city bathed in light.

Curiously, I had my sixteenth birthday dinner at Frank Baker's restaurant—now almost exactly half-a-lifetime ago. Birthday gift: Solomon 555 ski bindings and a down vest. The food: Frank Baker's buffet table—all the warm Jell-O you could eat. Michelle, Caroline, and Michael—do they remember as I do that silly, forgettable evening, back so long ago when we were all still young?

* * *

Recently there has been talk of tearing down Lions Gate Bridge, and such talk truly horrifies me. People speak of Lions Gate Bridge as being merely a tool, a piece of infrastructure that can be casually deleted, plundered from our memories with not a second thought to the consequences its vanishing might have on our interior lives.

I think that when people begin to talk like this, they are running scared—they are doing something that I know I do myself: I try to disguise what I am really feeling by saying and doing the opposite thing. The bridge is not merely a tool, not a casually deletable piece of infrastructure, and it can never be deleted from memories like an undesirable file.

I can't do this with Lions Gate Bridge anymore. Why was it so hard until recently for me to simply say that the bridge is a thing of delicate beauty—an intricate part of my life and memories? Why is it so hard for all of us to say loudly and clearly to each other that the bridge is an embodiment of grace and charm and we must not let it die?

Why would we destroy something we love rather than let a stupid pride prevent us from saying, "It means something to me"?

I never said what happened the night of the jumper.

After an hour or so, the jumper came down and was promptly whisked away by a screaming ambulance. Frank Baker came down off the roof of the Cadillac, took his bows to our claps, and he drove away.

I myself got back into my old Rabbit and drove across the bridge, but the bridge felt different that night, as though it led me to a newer, different place.

* * *

I want you to imagine you are driving north, across the Lions Gate Bridge, and the sky is steely grey and the sugar-dusted mountains loom blackly in the distance. Imagine what lies behind those mountains—realize that there are only more mountains—mountains until the North Pole, mountains until the end of the world, mountains taller than a thousand me's, mountains taller than a thousand you's.

Here is where civilization ends; here is where time ends and where eternity begins. Here is what Lions Gate Bridge is: one last grand gesture of beauty, of charm, and of grace before we enter the hinterlands, before the air becomes too brittle and too cold to breathe, before we enter that place where life becomes harsh, where we must become animals in order to survive.

This essay appeared originally in *Vancouver Magazine,* and then in a collection of small pieces published in 1996 called *Polaroids from the Dead.*

Seawall

Honey, let's dress in scary outfits and go watch the burning apartment building! The destruction of Englesea Lodge in 1981 marked a low point in terms of Vancouver's willingness to value or preserve its history.

What's also interesting in this photo is a snippet of the seawall, a 20 (or so) kilometre walkway that circles and loops around the city's watery shore. Starting at the Kits beach end, highlights include the citizens of Kits, the Maritime Museum (home of the *St. Roch*), Granville Island, the Olympic Village, Science World, the remnants of the old Expo site, beaches, the microclimate gardens of English Bay, Stanley Park, Lions Gate Bridge from below, spectacular views of the North Shore's industrial areas and amazing cityscape views. The seawall eventually takes you right into downtown to Canada Place and the city's two convention centres. It's the best five hours in town, two if you're on blades. And if you're a runner, perhaps your personal best.

Fred Herzog, *Fire, English Bay*, 1981, courtesy of Equinox Gallery

See-Throughs

In thirty years, most North American cities ought to be pretty much the same as they are now. The aura of Lincoln, Nebraska, will remain essentially untouched; Chicago will still be Chicago. Ditto Halifax, Tallahassee and what have you. A few new buildings, a few more people, bigger trees—you get the idea. But Vancouver? We have no idea what this place is going to be like next *year,* let alone in a few decades.

A case in point are what locals call "see-throughs," the glass condominium towers, pale blue or pale green, that have come to dominate the city skyline since 1990. They were built as contingency crash pads for wealthier Hong Kong citizens who were bracing themselves for the worst in the 1999 changeover of rule from England to China. The transition went smoothly, and thus the towers remain largely as empty as they appear. An occasional landlord will put those $19.99 white plastic stacking chairs out on balconies to generate the appearance of occupation, but these spaces are going cheap, cheap, cheap.

Ironically, these towers were designed for foreigners (and price-pointed at the exact same spot that the Canadian government required to accelerate a certain kind of immigration visa), but they've been discovered by locals who can't believe the quality of life available for surprisingly little money. The local elementary school filled up years ago. Nobody saw that coming.

These glass towers strike many visitors as a key element of the city's character. A friend from the States told his mother that Vancouver was a city of glass buildings and no curtains, and everybody gets to watch each other. A voyeur's paradise, so to speak. To Vancouverites, these towers signify a few things: the power of global history to affect our lives, and the average citizen's alienation from the civic political process—they're large glass totems that say "F-you" to us. At the same time, these towers symbolize a New World breeziness and a gentle desire for social transparency—a rejection of class structures and hierarchy. Regardless of any of that, it takes only a few weeks to build a see-through. Citizens go away on holiday and return to a completely different place. If only the people who build see-throughs could be in charge of the city's roadworks.

Fred Herzog, *Granville Street from Granville Bridge,* 1966, courtesy of Equinox Gallery

Lest we get too sentimental for the recent past, let's remember its air pollution and its visual pollution. Please note the blackened roof of the Hotel Vancouver—and thank you, large red sign, for telling us what the building is! Back in the late sixties and early 1970s, Batman and Mr. Burns time-shared the hotel's attic area as a pied-à-terre when visiting the city.

Pages 128-29: Fred Herzog, *Granville/Robson,* 1959, courtesy of Equinox Gallery
Above   Fred Herzog, *Four Billboards, Davie Street,* 1962, courtesy of Equinox Gallery

SkyTrain

Vancouver is very young, and its lifespan overlaps the evolution of the automobile, so it was designed around the car. Public transportation remains a marginal topic owing to the local sensibility that car ownership equals citizenship. Bike riders joyously fight this love-my-car notion during their random but massive "ride-ins," which cripple the city's bridges during rush hour. A month ago I saw a nude ride-in crossing the Burrard Street Bridge, and it must be noted for the record that even for the buffest and sveltest of bike riders, the hunched over position demanded by bicycles is not very, well, *flattering*.

In spite of the city's entrenched get-me-there-in-a-car-or-don't-get-me-there-at-all mentality, Vancouver has a ... monorail! Just like in *The Simpsons*. It's called SkyTrain, and it really does work, provided you live and work along its corridor. There's also the SeaBus, which tootles back and forth between North Vancouver and downtown. Sometimes I'll take it for no other reason than that I feel a need to be marine without much outlay of cash or effort. It's a peaceful happy ride, and the best way to grasp the city's scale and nautical feel.

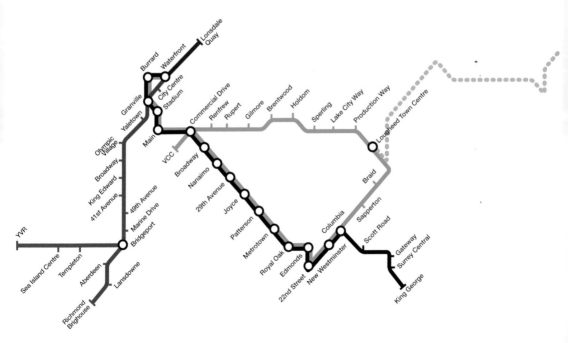

SkyTrain stations are notable for their architectural innovation.

Stanley Park

Stanley Park is named after Lord Stanley, some dead English guy who, it turns out, had never even visited Vancouver when the park was officially opened in 1888, back when the English really started pillaging the place. A year later he deigned to visit briefly—wooee! Note: for what it's worth, the Stanley Cup is also named after the man. Anyway, all of this aside, Stanley Park is one of a kind in the world ...

Stanley Park was logged about a hundred years ago, but all of the trees have grown back since then. If you think those trees are tall, look for the hundred-year-old stumps as broad as your kitchen floor and try to imagine what the *first-growth* forest was like. The park also once contained a zoo, which was reclassified as an animal prison in the 1990s and removed. Its aquarium is world renowned and features five beluga whales, one of which I was lucky enough to feed and pat on the nose a few years back, and its skin felt like the world's biggest wettest hard-boiled egg. Another fun fact: a two-minute clip of the aquarium's otters holding hands while floating on their backs on a sunny day is one of the all-time most Youtube'd videos.

Once, after having watched the belugas romp and the otters play, I came into the tropical section and saw millions of electric blue little fish; I had a good little cry because I was just swamped with the idea of how beautiful the world is. The place can do that to you.

Sometimes it's just nice to walk, ride or 'blade around the 8.5-kilometre (5.5-mile) seawall and then grab a cherry Popsicle from the snack bar at Lost Lagoon. I once had some photos taken of me standing naked in Beaver Lake in the park's centre, because on a sunny day with all the water lilies, it seemed like heaven, and the photographer wanted to take a transcendental-looking photo. My mother hates the photo, but I really love it; and best of all, I caught a turtle during the shoot.

Every year, somebody or some group comes up with a worthy project which will only take up "just a little bit of the park," but if all such schemes had come to pass, Stanley Park would have vanished decades ago. In the end, what we want there is *nothing*—just the trees and animals. As it should be.

The Storm

On December 15, 2006, a freakishly large storm passed through Vancouver (thank you, global warming), causing considerable damage to the city and its suburbs. But the big shocker was that the storm obliterated the western edge of the park, wiping out three thousand hundred-year-old trees as quickly and thoroughly as the Siberian Tunguska explosion of 1908. The park was closed for a few days after the storm, and the moment it reopened five days later, I visited it with friends. We and everyone else walked around in a daze, unable to process the extent of the decimation. Trees as wide as a four-door sedan were snapped off like satay skewers. It was a clear-cut. The one thing that everyone said, friends to friends and strangers to strangers, is how relieving it was that it was nature, not people, who caused the damage. Or did we?

There are many Vancouverites who've yet to see the damage. Two years later I was driving my mother downtown, and she asked to go through the park. Upon witnessing the devastation, she said, "Well, it's not all that bad, and just look at all the terrific new peekaboo views of West Vancouver."

My one beef with the City of Vancouver is why they don't have large billboards placed in that portion of the park explaining why it is that tourists who expected to see a magnificent treed jungle instead find a clear-cut. How hard can it be to do that?

Stó:lō

Vancouver originally had not one but many names given to it by its first residents, the Stó:lō Nation, but most Vancouverites didn't know this until recently.

By the same token, the Queen Charlotte Islands up north are called Haida Gwaii, which makes good sense, as the Haida were the first folks there. I heard somebody on the radio once say, "Who the hell was Queen Charlotte?" Good question—and so Haida Gwaii it is.

Growing up in Vancouver, you end up with a slightly schizoid relationship with First Nations cultures. In elementary school, you colour totem poles and make Haida-style masks. Years go on, and everywhere you look, Native motifs are splashed about. You're told, "This is your culture, this is part of your heritage." But then you get older and realize that, well, it's actually somebody else's heritage, and you have no claim to it at all. This makes you feel queasy about the time people spent making you think it was your own culture. And if First Nations culture isn't part of your heritage, then what should be your relationship with it? Do you respectfully keep your distance? Do you try and get involved? And what are you to make of the crowds who flock to stare at the totem poles at Stanley Park?

Native land rights are probably the biggest issue facing the province of B.C., let alone Vancouver. Unlike the U.S. and other parts of Canada, we never fought any major wars with the First Nations peoples, nor were there any treaties—land simply got taken.

Like most North American cities, Vancouver's place names derive from First Nations words. Above, we see how the name "Coquitlam," a local suburb, would look using modern orthographic spelling.

A sculpture by artist Brian Jungen, *Prototype for New Understanding #5,*
Nike Air Jordans, hair, 1999

Top 100 Surnames in Vancouver

1	LEE	18	SINGH	35	THOMPSON
2	WONG	19	LIU	36	SCOTT
3	CHAN	20	WILLIAMS	37	NGUYEN
4	SMITH	21	NG	38	CHENG
5	KIM	22	WU	39	ZHANG
6	CHEN	23	HO	40	YU
7	GILL	24	CAMPBELL	41	STEWART
8	LI	25	CHOW	42	YANG
9	BROWN	26	MACDONALD	43	SIDHU
10	JOHNSON	27	MILLER	44	SANDHU
11	WANG	28	CHANG	45	WHITE
12	WILSON	29	HUANG	46	PARK
13	LEUNG	30	LIN	47	ROBINSON
14	ANDERSON	31	CHEUNG	48	MOORE
15	LAM	32	MARTIN	49	DHALIWAL
16	JONES	33	LAU	50	CLARK
17	TAYLOR	34	YOUNG	51	MITCHELL

52	TANG	69	BAKER	86	LEWIS
53	WALKER	70	EVANS	87	LIM
54	MCDONALD	71	ROBERTSON	88	CLARKE
55	ROSS	72	KING	89	PHILLIPS
56	JOHNSTON	73	BELL	90	YEUNG
57	REID	74	DAVIS	91	HILL
58	GREWAL	75	LO	92	NELSON
59	CHU	76	GRAHAM	93	DAVIES
60	MA	77	WOOD	94	MURRAY
61	THOMAS	78	FRASER	95	GRANT
62	HALL	79	ROBERTS	96	BRAR
63	LAI	80	HARRIS	97	MORRISON
64	CHUNG	81	WATSON	98	TRAN
65	WRIGHT	82	PETERS	99	FUNG
66	CHOI	83	FRIESEN	100	HAMILTON
67	DHILLON	84	TAM		
68	JACKSON	85	MANN		

Trees

Vancouver's relationship with trees is a big one. One of the first things that people notice about Vancouver is how green the place is. The city is blessed with a temperate climate, which allows for the growth of everything from palm trees to alpine novelties such as lichen and edelweiss. The city drips with green, and in April and May, the city's rhododendrons, plums, cherries, azaleas and magnolias transform the city. The streets become aflutter with mounds of pink fluff snow, and everyone takes a deep breath and remembers exactly why they live here. It is glorious.

In Vancouver, you have to differentiate between trees and logging—two entirely separate things. B.C. generates one job per logged tree; the Americans generate three. Something is wrong here, and nobody wants to fix it, but that's another rant. Pretty much every bit of land visible from the city was logged at the turn of the century. What looks like primordial forest is second growth, not to be frowned on, but real trees have to be a thousand or so years old to truly rate.

In 1995 when I was in Europe, I located one of the continent's (then) three Touch-Tone phones and checked my messages. One was from my mother, who had been contacted by the Vancouver Police Department: "Hi dear. Mom here. Constable So-and-So from the police department called and asked if you'd parked your car inside the Hollow Tree before you left for Europe. I said I didn't think you had, but then I never know with you. Anyway, if you could please give him a call at ... " It turned out that my old VW Type-3 Fastback had been stolen by two hosers who'd driven around and gotten sloshed in it, but not before they'd strapped moose antlers onto the hood where the little VW crest is supposed to go. Afterward, they parked the car inside the Hollow Tree in Stanley Park and passed out, with bottles of scotch in their laps. I mention this because Vancouver is perhaps the only city in the world where criminals might strap moose antlers to the hood of a stolen car and park it inside a thousand-year-old hollow tree. And to my mother, I ask the question: Is my life really so weird that you might not be sure if I parked my car inside the Hollow Tree before going to Europe?

The Hollow Tree now leans precariously; its future is in endless debate.

Vansterdam

I get my share of people visiting Vancouver from all over the world, and I used to try to make up a list of Worthy Destinations to drive them around to see. These days, I don't bother, as sooner or later they all want to scurry off to the strip clubs, hemp bars or God-only-knows-what. I'll be in the car about to show them a pamphlet from the Museum of Anthropology and, suddenly, they're ... gone.

Quite often, guests will even know the names and details of which club they specifically want to visit. When I comment on their knowledge, the usual response is, "I visit their website every day!" The Museum of Anthropology brochure goes back into the glove compartment where it will undoubtedly yellow further. Guests are wished an amusing evening and instructed to cab back to the hotel.

The New York Times calls Vancouver "Vansterdam," because of its Dutch laxity on the issues of sex and pot. Exotic dancers, male and female, need not wear nipple tassels, pasties or G-strings. Nobody's really sure what the pot laws are, but there seem to be an awful lot of very funky-looking people roaming the streets.

The majority of Vancouverites are only dimly aware of the depth and breadth of what goes on here. This attitude mimics that of the Dutch, who may or may not like some of what goes on in Amsterdam, but it's all a part of living in a free society.

All of this sex and pot and whatever can sometimes create nasty scenarios—boundaries blur, freedoms are abused and all the rest of it. However, the American zero-tolerance strategy on these sorts of things is viscerally abhorrent, so things are unlikely to change too much in the near future. Party on, cab home and spare us the details.

Page 159 Christi Brinks at Brandi's Show Lounge

Victoria

Vancouverites typically visit Victoria once every three years, less often than they visit Seattle, because the trip to Vancouver Island is more complex and expensive than simply driving down the I-5. Psychologically one must also pass through what is locally known as "the tweed curtain." It's not just a folksy myth propagated by the city's tourism bureau: Victoria is kind of stuffy and English in a way that even England isn't any more.

In general, you always visit Victoria with the faint hope that when you get there, things will be slightly, well, *different* than the last time you were there. And, of course, the city remains impervious to change; this, on a deeper level, accounts for its subtle allure.

Victoria is British Columbia's capital and part of its quiet aura stems from the reluctance to change that is entrenched in bureaucratic environments. The irony here is that, as a province, B.C. tends to elect charismatic bumpkins of all parties into office, our secret belief being that the godawful situation left in the wake of the most recently ousted charismatic bumpkin is so horrific that it can only magically be fixed by yet another charismatic bumpkin. We keep on doing it, and we seem unable to stop ourselves.

Victoria is also a *huge* retirement destination for many Canadians, and as such has really amazing English-y antiques: military stuff, pewter and stamp collections—if that's your bag. What happens is that Aunt Eileen from Halifax or Windsor moved to Victoria to retire, had a lovely retirement and then died; the family phones up the lawyers and says, "Just sell it all."

There's a great used bookshop in Palo Alto, California, and I always wondered where they got such good stuff. Then I saw the owner in Victoria, and she was cleaning out a shop. So now I know.

In Grade 11, our class went on a field trip to Victoria to see the wildlife dioramas in the Royal British Columbia Museum. I ducked out with two friends. We walked over to the Parliament Buildings and asked to meet the then-provincial premier, and the people in his office said, sure. So we all had a nice chat about the honorary gifts lining the walls of his office—a fleece from New Zealand and swords from somewhere else, that kind of thing. And then we left. It's hard to imagine popping into, say, the Sacramento capitol buildings and doing the same thing—or any other capital city. There's something kind of nice to be said for remoteness.

Weather

In Vancouver, we don't get weather so much as *weathers.* In the span of a day, citizens can expect torrential downpours followed by balmy sunshine followed by ominous overcast followed by a killer sunset and finished with a mist. One is only allowed to whine if it's been raining for sixty consecutive days.

Last August I had to replace my roof, August being the only sure-thing warm weather month of the year. Wrong. The entire house sat beneath a huge plastic tent for six weeks of continual rainfall that ended the moment the roof was completed.

Vancouver's gift from global warming is that our weather has become more extreme. We may get the same amount of rainfall as ever, but it's spaced out differently ... droughts followed by deluges. And the storms in winter have become much more intense (see page 141).

To complain about the weather is the sure mark of an outsider. If you like blizzards and three-day springtimes and all of that, an entire continent beckons you. Vancouver's rain, while plentiful, is almost always fairly gentle, and it's not the bone-chilling monsoons of elsewhere. Seasons? No, we don't get New England's fall panorama, but we *do* get the most spectacular springs on the continent, where all the trees and shrubs go berserk with colour in a way reminiscent of Polynesia. And besides, in New England, once all those leaves have fallen, you've got only branches to look at for the next six months. Here, it stays green.

Umbrellas are vaguely permissible, but they *are* kind of dweeby, and besides, why aren't you wearing a hooded anorak or a fleece garment, anyway?

The West End

The West End is the large cluster of anonymous-looking concrete buildings which begins at Lost Lagoon and ends at Burrard Street; it has downtown on one side and English Bay on the other. Many Vancouverites spend a little bit of their youth in a West End apartment, which usually contains a futon, an intercom buzzer (with your name in white letters on a little black board outside the lobby), and wafer-thin walls and airless hallways that reek of somebody else's cooking or most recent cologne purchase.

The West End is for many a rite of passage. Most of the buildings were built during that brief but magic two-week period in 1964 when Suzanne Pleshette ruled the silver screen and Lester B. Pearson promised a better tomorrow. Some buildings are gems, some are dumps, and everybody's landlord is great except your own, who's always a psycho. Most buildings have NO PETS policies, yet it's a rare building that doesn't house more cats than humans.

There's also an urban legend that the West End has North America's highest population density—maybe it's true, but then Mexico City does spring to mind. But if it *is* the highest density of people on the continent, you'd never know it to walk though the West End's sleepy, quiet little roads, where people of all stripes wend their way. In the past week alone, while passing through the area's shaded streets, I've seen a lumberjack carrying a huge spray of tulips, a granny pensioner in black leather barrelling down sidewalks in her tiny electric cart, and a man dressed in dance clothes, with a bounce in his step, carrying a 4-litre can of purple latex.

Anthropological note: Because there are so many towers all close together, sooner or later one person's latent voyeurism meets with somebody else's latent exhibitionism, and many residents are made happy at very little cost.

And also, should you want a preview of heaven, I suggest you have drinks in the revolving restaurant at the top of the Empire Landmark, about thirty minutes before sundown. You'll gasp.

Whales

A few years ago I was driving downtown when I heard on the radio that a dead grey whale had washed up in English Bay. Without further thought, I drove there to see it. It was mid-afternoon on a glorious Technicolor blue sky day, and already a fair crowd had gathered around what, from a distance, appeared to be a fishing boat or a yacht lying on its side.

Up close the whale's skin was charcoal grey and covered in barnacles like a boat's hull, or like Deck Kote marine paint. Local marine biologists were there taking samples to try and figure out why the whale had beached itself. From the head they'd cut a square chunk of tissue the size, thickness and shape of a sofa cushion. It was orange and flaky looking, like a tin of canned salmon. In the open mouth, I could see the whale's baleen—the thin fibrous strands it used to filter out larger objects. It looked like a wiry broom, like an antique Japanese comb.

What really struck me was who'd come to see the whale—people who'd been working at their desks or photocopying or having meetings, who'd maybe heard about the whale while in the cafeteria listening to the local AM news station, and then suddenly dropped everything and scurried off to see it. Men wore ties; women were dressed in their office clothes. Everybody was scrambling over rocks coated with razor-sharp blue mussels and barnacles. One woman had snagged her pantyhose on a piece of driftwood; another had lost the heel of her shoe; one guy had stepped in a tidal pool and soaked his leather brogues, but I'll bet you a million bucks none of them cared.

The experience with the whale was so vivid that I wrote it into a movie set in Vancouver that I was writing, and to the director's credit, he nailed the moment perfectly.

The upshot, I guess, is that whales are sacred in Vancouver. Go into the beluga whale chamber at the Vancouver Aquarium and watch the communion between man and beast—it's real. It's undeniable. Even the most driven graffiti vandal won't deface one of the painted "whale wall" murals that cover many of the city's spaces.

When non-Vancouverites make passé quips about the "Save the Whales" slogan, Vancouverites think, "What—you want to *kill* the whales then?" Ecocynicism is a one-way ticket out of town.

Continuing from page 7, here we see the glamorous Steph Song who, like others in the scene, heard about the beached whale and came to see it for herself. What was magic about it when I went to see the whale that actually did land on the beach was that people came from their offices, and there were all these people in business shoes walking on the sand.

Whistler

Whistler, ninety minutes north of downtown, was a sleepy ski community back in the 1960s and 1970s. Now it's a sprawling, theme-parky mega-industryplex of a town, which came as surprise to nearly everybody. It wasn't just the town that got bigger—the price of a ski weekend got equally big. Much of Vancouver's population is simply priced out. Solace can be found in the fact that three excellent mountains exist within a thirty-minute drive from downtown—Cypress Mountain, Grouse Mountain and Mount Seymour—and all offer splendid night skiing, something which Whistler lacks.

A large part of Whistler's social texture comes from its labour pool, which shifts with the seasons. It's highly transient and almost entirely youthful, largely fuelled by Eastern Canadians, Australians and New Zealanders harbouring (it really must be said) outdoorsy fantasies of consequence-free sex, drugs and downhill skiing. For the first-time visitor, the smell of pheromones, marijuana and Piz Buin can be overwhelming, and for the young industry workers, it's indeed almost irresistible. And the fact remains, the resort does have some of the world's best skiing.

There aren't too many people who live in Whistler year-round—only about ten thousand people who might plausibly be deemed as "locals." Yet for the transient labour pool, nirvana is passing as a local. If you want to be adored in Whistler Village, simply say to someone, "Hey you look like a local—how can I find … "

Both the men and the women of Whistler complain about the lack of long-term commitment in the regional dating pool. A friend of mine, Stephanie, a Toronto transplant, recently said to me, "If I meet one more guy with a pickup truck and a dog who's only looking for something casual, I seriously think I'm going to go mental." But of course, almost nobody's local, almost everybody's a transient and the possibility of commitment approaches zero—but it's that one in a million chance that keeps 'em all coming.

Wildlife

The mountains around Vancouver were logged at the dawn of the 20th century, and it's only been in the last decade that canopy growth and undergrowth have allowed for the resurgence of mammalian megafauna. Growing up on the North Shore, I spent entire summers in the woods without even a raccoon or skunk. Things have changed.

Last summer a black bear cub ambled down my driveway and paused outside the kitchen window. It put its tongue onto the gravel and licked up some sunflower seeds left there for the birds. It then wagged its tongue back and forth to shake away the gravel, and swallowed the seeds. The winter's alpine snowfall had been deep, the berries usually favoured by bears hadn't ripened, and so the animals roamed the suburbs, foraging for any food they could find. My visitor then ran up a back retaining wall and proceeded to snooze beneath my apple tree. The police, when I phoned, said that it was best to do nothing. "Whatever you do," they warned, "don't feed the bear. A fed bear is a dead bear." Did we learn nothing from Yogi Bear cartoons?

Other species invade Vancouver's inhabited areas with casual frequency— coyotes, deer, and skunks and raccoons in droves. Cougars, justifiably wary, stay on the fringes and are only spotted infrequently. All of these animals are out there, up in the mountains, and they can see the city as clearly as we can see the mountains. What must they make of us? I doubt that they consider us some sort of meat-flavoured Popsicle. Truth be told, they probably think of us as big, noisy insects that attack without even being provoked. We all like to see ourselves as a St. Francis of Assisi, but self-flattery is all too human. Let's face it, we're the pests.

Wreck Beach

Wreck Beach is the nakedest place in Canada, located 75 metres (250 feet) below the westernmost bluffs out at the University of British Columbia. In summer, thousands of solar enthusiasts (and even a few in winter, too) go there to simply lie on the beach and get natural. That's it. No weirdness. No anarchy. No untoward friskiness. Just the sun. Beach-goers stake their claims using one of the hundreds of logs which have escaped the enormous log booms nearby (quite a sight in themselves). It's interesting to see how asexual, or rather, asexy, people become when everybody's in their birthday suits *en masse.*

Near Wreck Beach are gun turret towers built during WW2 to ward off a supposed Japanese invasion. Many a Vancouver youth has frittered away a Friday night in these glamorously decrepit spots, watching the sun set, smoking hand-rolled cigarettes and discussing whether or not the Earth is like an electron and the sun like a nucleus, and ... so forth.

YVR

For many people, YVR is where Vancouver begins and ends. Personally, I spend way too much time in airports and over the years have become an accidental critic on the subject—so it gives me a boosterist little jolt of pride to say that YVR is pretty well the best airport going. Aside from the fact it operates smoothly and serenely, it also offers the air traveller a crash course in Vancouver style: smooth river rock; stone from Whistler; glass, glass, glass; teal- and grey-coloured carpets and textiles; cedar woodwork; and best of all, a truly stunning gathering of West Coast Native art. Had the airport been done incorrectly, it could have been a sort of Disney version of Vancouver style. But, thinking about it, that might be impossible to do. Vancouver is one of the few cities going that are bucking the trend toward homogenization and pasteurized global taste. It's a fractal city—a city of no repeats. It's unique, and it's my home. So if you're arriving, welcome; and if you're on your way out, return again soon, and just think of how good the rain was to your complexion and how green the world truly is.